Your
Dream of
Recovery

Your Dream of Recovery

Dream Interpretation and the 12 Steps

by
Shelly Marshall

A.R.E. Press • Virginia Beach • Virginia

A.R.E. Press
Sixty-Eighth & Atlantic Avenue
P.O. Box 656
Virginia Beach, VA 23451-0656

Library of Congress Cataloging-in-Publication Data
Marshall, Shelly, 1948- .
    Your dream of recovery : dream interpretation and the 12 steps / Shelly Marshall.
        p.   cm.
    Includes bibliographic references and index.
    ISBN 0-87604-332-5
    1. Dream interpretation. 2. Dreams—Therapeutic use. 3. Twelve-step programs. 4. Cayce, Edgar, 1877-1945. I. Title.
BF1091.M346 1995
154.6'34—dc20

                                                                                94-40522

Cover design by Jennifer Heyd Wharton

Dedication

This book is dedicated to Elsie Sechrist, whose understanding and presentation of dream interpretation in *Dreams: Your Magic Mirror* touched my spirit and influenced the whole course of my recovery from alcoholism/addiction.

Included in this dedication is my mother, Jo Gerulis, who introduced me to the Edgar Cayce material and to recovery in the 12-Step programs which, without both, would have altered the course of my entire life.

Table of Contents

Preface

Like a rare gem, the many facets of spirituality in America shimmer and sparkle in every direction imaginable. The various facets can be as conservative as Amishism, as traditional as Catholicism or Buddhism, or as radical as Scientology. Our spiritual foundations can be as disciplined as yoga and as mystical as dream interpretation; as old as the pyramids along the Nile and as young as our first waking breath every morning that signifies our search for God anew each day.

One of the largest spiritual movements in Western society in this century began on June 10, 1935, with the founding of Alcoholics Anonymous—a way of life anchored on 12 Steps of moral conduct guided by an alignment with a power greater than the self. AA itself is actually based on the philosophy of the Oxford movement, which proclaimed that the "world could not change for the better until its citizens did."[1] To effect this change in individuals, followers were asked to live by absolute standards of behavior—honesty, purity, selflessness, and love. However, these standards of behavior were not considered rules, but simply guidelines by which followers could measure their conduct and spiritual progress.

Prior to the Oxford movement, dogmatic religious practices had been of only marginal help to winos, drunks, and barflies. At the same time, the medical profession had all but thrown up its hands in despair. But a former stockbroker and "hopeless" alcoholic, Bill Wilson, had managed some abstinence based on a spiritual awakening induced partly by his introduction to the Oxford group. Bill recognized that in living by the absolutes, he could rebuild his life without alcohol. Once he met Dr. Bob Smith, who also managed to recognize the value of this life style and stay sober, AA was born, although not originally known by that name.

Even though the absolute standards for behavior assented to by the Oxford movement certainly improved the lives of all who followed the path, early recovering drunks found it more expedient to break off and form their own groups, which soon became known as Alcoholics Anonymous. After three years of meeting and practicing the principles contained in the sober movement, the 12 Steps as we now know them were immortalized in the book, *Alcoholics Anonymous.*

By the 1970s people, in general, realized that the 12-Step approach to life was a good idea for anyone in search of healing for addictions and inner struggles of all kinds. These programs began springing up all over the world. Karen Green writes in *12 Steps Illustrated* that 12-Step fellowships "are a circle of recovery for millions of individuals in an expanding universe of mutual support groups. Alcoholics Anonymous, Adult Children of Alcoholics, Overeaters Anonymous, Gamblers Anonymous, and Narcotics Anonymous address but the tip of an iceberg of addictions."[2] She goes on to explain that each week from fifteen to twenty million people attend over half a million 12-Step support groups in America alone and that over 100 other countries host 12-Step programs.

From this flourishing movement, a new societal mentality has emerged on the use of spiritual methodology for improving and mending lives. Professionals, as well as the whole country, can see that the scourge of the earth, the lowest of the low, the alcoholic wretch can recover through a program based on spiritual principles. Most surprising, it is a program based not on any one religion, but on an open-minded, principled life style.

The 12-Step approach to life relies on a universal and principled code of behavior rather than dogmatic codes of "sin and not sin." The belief structure supporting it is personal, multivariant, and (with few exceptions) a matter of choice. Since spiritual or God-conscious principles are universal, people practicing the 12 Steps often find themselves paralleled in their spiritual pursuits with the principles associated with metaphysical thought.

So deeply has this association formed between 12-Step advocates and metaphysical thinkers, that many 12-Step or "recovery" stores have combined their inventory with the metaphysical; book distributors often specialize in "recovery" *and* "new age." Many 12-Step group members have discovered the *Search for God* books (based on information from Edgar Cayce, this country's greatest mystic and dream consultant) and the *Course in Miracles* (a book purported to have been inspired by Christ on how to obtain spiritual wholeness) as other focal points in their never-ending quest for progress.

For numerous people in the program a significant aspect of blending "recovery" and "metaphysical" pursuits for alignment with spiritual guidance naturally embraces the tools of prayer and meditation from the 12 Steps and dream interpretation from the metaphysical domain. After all, dreams have been guiding, chiding, and warning humans since the dawn of our consciousness here on earth. The symbols in dreams help reflect the future and mirror the inner self. From the "dream time" of the aborigines to Carl Jung's collective unconscious, we have come to learn that dreams can aid us in many ways. As many in the program are discovering, dreams can forge a path toward a spirituality so rich that we can reach dimensions in our growth heretofore unrealized.

This text is a manual for expanding our 12-Step work by adding the dimension of dream guidance. In Part I of this text, we (myself and you) will examine the world presented to us in our dreams. We will learn how to apply the knowledge gained therein to improve our understanding and application of the principles we learn in our 12-Step studies. In chapter 1, we will discuss the philosophy of dreaming for recovery and the possible obstacles we might encounter in the attitudes of society about metaphysical explorations. In chapters 2 and 3 we will learn how to interpret dream symbology and transform interpretations into meaningful messages to apply to our lives. We will explore the usefulness of not only interpreting dreams, but our visions and life events as well. I will also introduce you to "Your Dreamwork Glossary" and give you instructions for creating your own glossary while learning to interpret symbols. Chapter 4 explores the joys of beginning a 12-Step dreamwork group and outlines the procedures for such.

Part II is "Your Dreamwork Glossary" and provides a basis for understanding universal, cultural, and personal meanings for the symbols you will find in your dreams, visions, and life events. It is divided into segments based on the different categories of the symbols we find in our dreams. "Your Dreamwork Glossary" is designed in these segments for ease in recording symbols and will enable you to author the best dream dictionary in the world—*yours!*

In Part III we will examine dreams from members of various 12-Step fellowships so that you gain firsthand knowledge of how dream interpretation and 12-Step recovery works. I have gathered hundreds of dreams from program people in the U.S., Canada, England, the Ukraine, and Russia. We will use some of them to illustrate, point by point, symbol by symbol, how dreams aid us in our spiritual growth.

The 12 Steps to a spiritual life are not achieved in a moment; they are applied and refined over a lifetime. Dreams can be of immense value in understanding, working, and gauging our progress with each of them. Bill Wilson, who founded AA and consequently became the father of all 12-Step programs, said that as important to anything else in recovery was his discovery that spiritual principles would solve all his problems. And Edgar Cayce, the great mystic and dream consultant, said, "Harken to thy dreams and visions, for these may oft be channels through which . . . the choice [can be] made for the better universality in the activities."[3]

As this book unfolds, we will discover the universality of the guidance in our dreams and apply it to our spiritual programs in ways so enriching that we will be rocketed into a new dimension of spirituality chock-full of serenity, contentment, and usefulness to ourselves and our fellow human beings.

Acknowledgments

Grateful acknowledgment is made for permission to reprint the following material:

Excerpts from *Alcoholics Anonymous* reprinted by permission of Alcoholics Anonymous World Services, Inc.

The 12 Steps and the 12 traditions are reprinted and adapted from the original texts published by Alcoholics Anonymous World Services, Inc. (AA). Reprinting or adaptation of this material does not mean that AA has reviewed or approved the contents of this publication, nor that AA agrees with the views expressed herein. AA is a program of recovery from alcoholism only—use of the 12 Steps in connection with programs and activities which are patterned after AA, but which address other problems, does not imply otherwise.

Usage of the Edgar Cayce Readings

The Association for Research and Enlightenment, Inc. (A.R.E.), is a membership organization for those interested in the study and use of the Cayce readings.

For reference purposes and to preserve anonymity, each person who received a reading was given a number, and the reading carries that number instead of the name of the person. For example, reading number 3902-2 was given for the person assigned number 3902. This particular reading was the second one that person obtained from Cayce, as indicated by the "-2" following the reading number.

PART I

DREAMING FOR RECOVERY

1

Dreaming for Recovery

I didn't really know which lounge I was in again. They had all begun to resemble each other after a while. I was seated at the piano bar, with the usual bar and grill behind me. At twenty-one years of age, I sat alone, swilling some concoction or other, and fancying myself to be very desirable to the pianist. His music didn't make sense to me; it wasn't harmonizing or I wasn't responding. The smoky surroundings reeked of grease, stale alcohol, and body odor. I was so drunk that my head flopped on the piano and I probably reeked of grease, stale alcohol, and body odor, too.

Suddenly, screaming erupted from the background. It seems that the grill and nearby area had caught fire. In an attempt to put it out, the cook panicked, dropping something very heavy on the edge of the grill. It flipped up, throwing a vat of burning grease across the room and directly landing on my back as I wallowed in my stupor.

My hair and back burst into flames, as well as a large portion of the room. Pandemonium ensued, but I didn't feel any pain or panic, just penetrating heat spreading down my head and spine. I decided not to fight it, however, and just let myself die. I simply gave up without a fight. It felt wonderful to let go of the woes of the world and maybe find peace at last.

My life quickly drained away and abruptly, without warning, I suddenly didn't want to die. As my life force faded, I instantaneously wanted it back. I jumped up, enveloped in flames, and spotted the door to the right of the pianist, so close, yet I wasn't sure I could make it. I was only sure, beyond a shadow of a doubt, that if I got through it, I would live.

Then I awoke. It had been so real that I could still feel the intense heat down my backside. I was sweaty and shaky and extremely grateful to be alive. "Whew, it was only a dream," you might say. But it was the first conscious heralding of the biggest change ever to occur in my life. It came only a week before I found sobriety by joining a 12-Step program for additional recovery.

Earlier that year, my mother had introduced me to the work of Edgar Cayce, who is sometimes called "the sleeping prophet." Cayce, considered to be America's best-documented psychic, gave over 14,000 psychic readings during a span of fifty years. He died in 1945, but during his life he had the ability to go into a trance-like state and deliver accurate information from the world beyond. His advice was so thorough, provocative, and well documented that it is hard not to think of him as anything *but* a prophet. From Mr. Cayce's trance-like state, he "read" people—gaining knowledge from their hidden soul records, auras, and dreams. It was his information on using dream interpretation for improving one's life that captivated first my mother, then me.

What was my brush with dream-death telling me? First, some background. Nearly everyone in my family is addicted to some form of mind-affecting chemical. The disease literally consumed us all, as happens in many families. I had been drinking and drugging since the age of fifteen and, during that time, not a twenty-four-hour period went by that I wasn't loaded on something. At twenty, I actually slept with a bottle of beer beside me. Not only did I frequent bars in my spare time, but I insisted on working in them so that I had a ready supply for my addiction. At one point, I was literally dying—puking green slime, which was also coming out the other end. I knew something was horribly wrong, but exactly what the cause of this terrible stress and struggle in my young life was confounded me. (Alcoholism in the young was not recognized in 1969.) I thought, as did my mother, that the work of this Edgar Cayce fellow that had helped so many others would be just the ticket to help me. And dream interpretation was the medium with which I began.

It just so happened that my mother had had a dream a few months earlier. In her dream she found herself walking down a long corridor, doors strung along both walls. Each door was labeled and, although Mom couldn't remember each one, upon awakening she did retain that one door was labeled "12 Steps," another labeled "School," another "Surgical Supplies," and one labeled "Old Soldier's Home." It turned out that this particular dream had revealed the next decade or so of her life and the meaning was not lost to her. Not only was the dream showing her the way to go in chronological order (Mom sobered up in a 12-Step program, went to school, became an x-ray technician, and later had the love of her life die in a veterans hospital), but this prophetic dream was reassuring her that her life (which at the time was an alcoholic mess) would be all right.

So, back to the bar and my sleeping reality. My dream came just several months on the tail of my mom's. It was showing me where my life was headed—*death!* The booze was destroying my sanity (stupor) by interfering with the harmony of my life (cannot understand the music); it was all consuming (engulfed in flames) and would literally kill me (I invited death and actually *felt* its touch), unless I escaped the drunkenness into sobriety (out from the burning bar through the door). This dream also signified my need for purification (flames expunging me) to enter a new life (through a door).

The final crisis in the dream was my ability to actually *feel* the death process—the life force leaving me—so what I had chosen for myself by not caring if I lived or died was revealed quite graphically. From the thunderbolt nature of the dream, I learned that I did indeed care—I wanted to live. It wasn't long before the choice of joining a 12-Step recovery program presented itself to me. Because of my dream (just as Mom had had her dream six weeks earlier), I was able to embrace sobriety with open arms and an open mind—thus began my use of dream interpretation with my 12-Step program.

Dreams as a Healing Mechanism

Although many experts and professionals in Western medicine consider dreams to be little more than mental anecdotes, not actual healing mechanisms, Carl Jung and later his followers recognize(d) the actual healing power of dreams in society's addictions. Marion Woodman, an internationally renowned Jungian psychotherapist, believes that addictions (from chemicals to diet disorders, workaholism, relationships, and even styles of thinking) are misguided attempts "to fill a spiritual void at the center of our lives with inappropriate 'remedies.' "[1] To addicts this spiritual void or hole represents a lack of spiritual concreteness and often faith. It is a form of denial with us—a denial of our spirituality. Woodman further states that to *step into that void* via the dream in order to meet our angels and devils is the process of creation and healing in our lives. We step into the void or hole to confront our denial (and fear) in order to embrace our spirituality and heal ourselves.

"It seems to me," adds Woodman, "that many addicts—and that includes most of us, for who in this culture is not an addict?—know at some level that we have to go into that hole. In dreams, repeatedly the dreamer is told there is a black hole; frightening, forbidding, but nevertheless we have to walk over the threshold and go into that hole. And often we say, 'No, I can't do it.' Sometimes it takes years before the dream says, 'Okay, now's the time, move!' And when it does, sometimes, as in a fairy tale, the dream takes us to a door or to a threshold. Sometimes, instead of following the dream, we back off and start running around the hole again."[2]

However, by combining the strength of our support groups with the practice of prayer and meditation, using dreams as an augmentation to our spiritual quest will help us enter that black hole, confront our spiritual denial, and heal all the more swiftly.

Although there may be some authoritative resistance from our churches and the medical profession to our using dreams as a means of spiritual healing, an understanding of their confusion and objections makes it possible for us to be comfortable with our own choices. We mustn't use others' objections as an excuse to drop this rich path of exploration and growth. Just as the richness of a 12-Step spiritual program can be lost on the uninitiated, so, too, can one lose the value of dream images and metaphors when refusing to step over the threshold into the void. This may occur because religion tells us that use of dreams is evil or science tells us it is paranormal rubbish. We will shortly enter a discussion about the merits of religious and scientific resistance to using dream interpretation and the 12-Step programs as a means to spiritual growth and fulfillment. First, I want to make clear something very important to the foundation of this discussion that I learned from my personal psychic named Robea.

Dreams: Our Heritage from God

Robea had joined Alanon (the spouse's counterpart to AA) as a result of marriage to a cocaine addict. Her spiritual growth in the program led her to a deep faith in herself and development of metaphysical abilities, so that she began supporting herself by offering psychic readings and psychic therapy—something she thought she could never do.

After a series of particularly horrendous ordeals in my life, in which I "foresaw" the events first in dreams and visions, I went to my psychic friend, a little frightened. Maybe, I thought, I was even a little bit crazy because others would certainly look at me askance if I mentioned my experiences. "Why me?" I lamented. "I don't know why I'm given this kind of information ahead of time. I don't want to have anything to do with this kind of stuff, much less predict it. Who am I anyway? A delusional person, God's chosen, or God's damned?"

Robea kept assuring me that these events, although horrible to me at the time, would be turned into the highest good of everyone involved by a merciful Higher Power. She said that my expanding abilities with dream understanding would only serve to help the process. It was nothing to fear. Indeed, I was finally able to come to terms with my own fears of psychic dream-and-vision abilities and *revealing those abilities to others* as a result of the ordeal.

"Shelly," she explained, "you're not *special* because you have these dreams and visions or *different* from others, nor *are you chosen* or any such thing. You are an ordinary human being seeking spiritual growth. Do you think the people in the Bible, the ones with miracles whom God or the angels spoke with, the ones who dreamed dreams for the future of their people, were any different from the rest of us? No, they were ordinary people in every sense of the word."

She told me to think of the widow Ruth gleaning grain in the fields and Boaz spotting her and taking her as his wife. Ruth's heritage placed her in the lineage to Jesus the Christ (Book of Ruth). Robea told me also to think of Joseph in Pharoah's prison after being sold into slavery by his brothers and then falsely accused of rape. From the dungeon, he was raised to the second highest position in the kingdom at the right hand of the Pharoah because of his ability to interpret dreams (Genesis 37-41). Robea mentioned the goatskin tanner and Pharisee, Saul, having a vision on the dusty road to Damascus; he later became Paul, a disciple of Christ (Acts 9).

"They were like us," she continued, "not somehow different and special." Her words made me think about how these biblical characters were carpenters, farmers, fishermen, rabbis, mothers, fathers—and how all the things that went on in their lives must be available in our lives. "It's not scary, special, different—it's life," Robea explained. "All the miracles, guardian angels, precognitive dreams, contact with God—all are available to each and every one of us, I promise you."

I recalled something I had read from one of Edgar Cayce's readings: "For, remember, the Infinite spoke oft to those He would warn, to those He would direct; and God is the same yesterday, today and forever."[3] I knew that Robea had spoken the truth and from that day forward my fear of any "special" or even "delusional" ability or insight no longer frightened me. These miraculous events happen to ordinary people, like me and like you. It is our heritage from God to have access to other realms of existence, not just the scientific world of the Aristotelian thinker.

Dreamwork and Christianity

An interesting depiction of dreamwork and how it came to be frowned upon by fundamentalist Christians is revealed in the book *Dreams and Spiritual Growth* by Louis M. Savary, Patricia H. Berne, and Strephon Kaplan Williams. The early Christians clearly had deep enthusiasm for dreams and dreamwork. Saint Augustine believed that God gives us dreams as gifts and that we should welcome them from the merciful, providential care of God.

However, Saint Jerome, a contemporary of Saint Augustine's, was the man responsible for helping throw dreams out of favor by the church, just as Aristotle and his "rational mind" position helped throw dreamwork out of favor with the intellectual. We know why Aristotle took a revisionist attitude toward dreams. He simply didn't believe in anything that one couldn't prove through one of the five senses.[4] But we'll probably never know why, in St. Jerome's preparation of the Latin translation of the Bible from Hebrew, he deliberately mistranslated "anan" (akin to witchcraft) into "observe dreams." Until the mid-twentieth century, Jerome's Latin Vulgate Bible was the standard by which most church officials taught. As a result, Leviticus 19:26 and Deuteronomy 18:10 read, "You shall not practice augury nor observe dreams," when they should have read, "You shall not practice augury nor witchcraft." For centuries church officials equated dreams with witchcraft and necromancy. Although Morton Kelsey in his book *God, Dreams, and Revelation* explained the mistranslation so that Bibles today may carry a more correct translation, the past stigma still prevails in many church teachings.

Becoming Your Own Dreamwork Authority

In addition, the problem of casting dreams in the light of witchcraft and other unscientific slapdash, there are still those who believe that the phenomenon of dreams is simply a product of the human mental condition and has no objective reality. Of course, there are those who suspect that religious beliefs have no objective reality, either. In addition, there are a number of inbetween variations, such as those who believe that *their* religious belief has an objective reality, but that the beliefs of others who believe differently don't.

Because of the widely growing interest in spiritual growth and the continuing fascination by the public for dreams, authorities are again giving some credence to dreamwork. Freud, in his book *The Interpretation of Dreams*, gave working with the subconscious much respectability, although he did not link it to the spiritual needs of humanity, but to dark pathological issues. He and many of his followers thought that they were bringing a new grasp of the dreamworld to humankind. But whereas laypeople may see purpose in the metaphors of their dreams, the Freudian approach is more likely to focus on repressed traumas and hidden blocks to mental health recovery. This may be somewhat justified, although pathological demons are only a minuscule part of a very large, sometimes complex, but rich well of guidance from an ever-expanding spiritual life.

In the paradigm of the mental health profession, psychologists and psychiatrists attempt to look for the meaning of the dream experience in the psyches of dreamers rather than to acknowledge that actual spiritual guidance is taking place. Aristotle denied that any divine guidance came through dreams. This present book not only acknowledges that dreams contain divine guidance, but it encourages readers to seek it as well. In a psychic reading given in 1932, Edgar Cayce said, "There has been, and ever when the physical consciousness is at rest, the other self communes with the *soul* of the body, see?"[5]

All conventional professionals are not to be spurned, though. We have some startlingly in-depth contributions to dreamwork by Jungian devotees such as Marion Woodman. Again—it is important for us to understand the concerns of the established professional so as not to be intimidated as we become our own dreamwork authorities. Just as I doubted at one time any genuine ability to foresee the future, the more I understood, the better equipped I was to believe in myself.

A prominent New York psychiatrist once told a reporter for *Omni* magazine that she didn't think laypeople had any business "stomping around in the unconscious." Her reasoning was that she and other authorities know best what is "really" going on there. Mainstream psychologists and psychiatrists will often treat (either with drugs or psychotherapy) our passage into other realms, but we can't expect them to believe in the reality of these realms. Such experiences are likely to be labeled as hallucinations.

It's all right, in their view, to use our dream symbols as analogies for personality disorders, childhood's repressed traumas, and the by-product of the beans we ate for dinner, but suggest that you possess precognition, have seen angels, or heard God's voice and you tread dangerously close to a diagnosis of schizophrenia. It reminds me of my favorite line from the work of Lily Tomlin, "How come when we talk to God it's called prayer, but when God talks to us it's called schizophrenia?"

We are, *must be*, our own experts. Dream interpretation does not require professional training. Could you imagine the Pharoah being told by the expert court advisers, "This Joseph is a layman. What does the imbecile know? He shouldn't be stomping around in your subconscious"? (Genesis 41:1-43) Or others calling Mary's visitation by an angel about a virgin birth an hallucination and locking her up for schizophrenia? (Luke 1:26-38) Or John the Baptist's father, Zechariah, being told that the loss and return of his speech coinciding with predictions from an angel of a son late in life (Luke 1:11-25, 57-64) labeled "conversion disorder"? We are ordinary people living in an extraordinary world, and our dreams can, do, and will guide our growth. It's not magic; it is a wonderland of opportunity for each and every one of us.

Dreamwork and Your 12-Step Program

This particular book will show you how to begin using dreams to enhance your spiritual growth, mainly through the 12 Steps. It will help you regardless of which 12-Step program you may be using. Although I will be quoting the book of *Alcoholics Anonymous*, known as the "Big Book," because it is the foundation upon which all the 12-Step programs are built, our dreamwork will in no way be limited to Alcoholics Anonymous, Narcotics Anonymous, or any of the direct offshoots of AA. There are now literally hundreds of 12-Step programs operating in the world. The issues people in recovery now deal with have become so varied and rich, we not only see programs for chemical dependency, but also for overeaters, gamblers, sex addicts, art addicts, repeat offenders, abusive parents, emotional problems, and various mental problems. The list of 12-Step spiritual recovery groups is phenomenal, and they exist to help everyday, ordinary people.

There are several things to remember when we are working with the 12-Step programs and dream interpretation. First, members of 12-Step programs look upon each Step, with its level of growth, as a rite of passage; there is no absolute dividing line between the recovering and the nonrecovering (unless maybe it is a slip back into addiction, which in itself can also be seen as another lesson or stepping-stone). Next, we in the fellowships do not think of our programs as a religion, nor do groups support any particular faith. There is no sense of religious dogma. We employ "approaches" to living a spiritual life and maintaining a spiritual path, which include meritorious action, moral responsibility, and a continuing search for God.

Our way of life addresses the *principles* by which we grow closer to God—known as our Higher Power in the 12-Step fellowships. Always, we stress in the 12-Step programs that we address God, *as we understand Him,* and in no way is this meant to infringe on or supersede the reader's belief system or personal search. We are not professional mental health workers, although our program works miracles in mental health. Likewise, this book is not the last word on dream interpretation, although this dreamwork can actually create miracles in your program.

Into a Higher Dimension of Recovery

Yes, we are everyday people who follow a simple program in order to overcome severe life problems by seeking to live spirituality-based, principled lives. A huge number of our people work a simple program based on the earth plane entirely, never going beyond into other realms. For them, it is enough. However, there are a significant number of us who find ourselves "rocketed into a fourth dimension," as referred to in the "Big Book" by Bill Wilson.[6]

And this is where dream interpretation emerges as one of the great tools we can use toward our spiritual growth. In *The Dream Book: Symbols for Self-Understanding,* author Betty Bethards talks about three free tools we can use. "The most valuable tools for helping us along in life are free and available to all: dreams, prayer, and meditation. If we would take advantage of these, much of the guesswork, confusion, and hardship of life would vanish."[7] The 12-Step program also relies heavily on the last two: prayer and meditation. In fact the 11th Step reads, "We sought through prayer and meditation to improve our conscious contact with God, *as we understood Him.*" It's not too far a stretch to imagine it written as, "We sought through prayer, meditation, *and dreams* to improve our conscious contact with God, *as we understood Him.*" And indeed for me, I work the 11th Step just this way.

Although the original "Big Book" doesn't talk about using dreams as a tool, it is no secret that the founder of the 12-Step approach, Bill Wilson, leaned heavily toward metaphysical philosophy and exploration. We must remember that *Alcoholics Anonymous* was written in the 1930s, when it would not have been wise to refer to much outside the domain of accepted scientific or religious thought. In fact, referring to God as our "Higher Power" and including all spiritual beliefs, even agnostics, for sanctified growth, recovery, and life was ground-breaking at the time.

Our 12-Step programs have naturally evolved, with their principled beliefs in honesty, open-mindedness, and willingness to learn, into a modern creative spirituality able and willing to explore other realms. Many metaphysical bookstores also carry 12-Step material and vice versa. Even book distributors who specialize in the metaphysical often create a second special category for recovery books.

So the alliance has been formed between the 12-Step spiritual approach to recovery and the metaphysical search for God. It is interesting to note that Edgar Cayce, our modern-day precursor into this age of heightened spiritual awareness, believed that the healing of all ailments had to include one's spiritual attributes and applications in life. The importance of prayer and meditation were also greatly emphasized by him, in addition to using the inner guidance we receive via dreams. Author Reba Ann Karp, in *The Edgar Cayce Encyclopedia of Healing*, reports that Cayce believed that "Treatment [for addictions] at the mental-spiritual level was given as much importance as physical measures."[8] And we can easily compare this to the AA philosophy which clearly states that "When the spiritual malady is overcome, we straighten out mentally and physically."[9]

I always delight in remembering the story of Cayce walking with a friend and spotting two men working with a drunk. They were "12th-Stepping," which is the part of our program that requires us to work with others who suffer from our same ailment. Cayce psychically "read" their auras and remarked on the true spiritual nature of a program that was built on service. That story always warms my heart, thinking that Cayce in some way recognized and validated our program in its early stages.

Where Do Dreams Come From?

In its simplest form, the 12-Step program asks us to:
Examine ourselves and be honest (Steps 1, 4, 8, and 10)

Trust and rely on God (Steps 2, 3, 6, and 11)
Take meritorious and moral action (Steps 5, 7, 9, and 10)
Be of service to others (Step 12)

Although we will make progress in all these areas just by working the 12 Steps, we will work them better, deeper, more meaningfully once we learn to use the guidance from our dreams. Dreams actually come from varied sources—the many levels of our own subconscious, our Higher Power, our higher self, our guides, and what is known as the akashic record.

What is important to remember is that just as our 12-Step programs stress *God, as we understand Him*, each of these dream sources will be *as you understand it.* Our own subconscious can represent our imaginations, our psyches, our biological DNA imprints, or our conscious repressions. Our Higher Power can be God, the Spirit of Nature, Light, Allah, Jesus Christ, the universal mind, the Force, or the Fellowship. Our higher self can be our eternal soul, our Christ Consciousness, our moral consciousness, superconsciousness, or our ethereal mind. Our guides can be guardian angels, saints, departed relatives, allies, celestial beings, or—if you believe—even aliens and other dimensional beings. Although "the akashic record" generally refers to a belief that all thought and action is permanently recorded in the cosmos, we can think of it as the Book of Life, the connection between all souls, or the collective unconscious.

As we discuss dream symbols and sources, we will be using a myriad of terms. Each reader has the freedom to view these sources as they fit into his or her spiritual beliefs. Remember that dreamwork is just as open to esoteric interpretation as our 12-Step programs are.

Dreams contain such a wealth of information that there hasn't been a period from the ancient "dreamtime" of the aborigines to the Old Testament times of profound dream visions to modern-day psychiatrists probing into the subconscious that didn't give some credence to the images that populate our sleep. Dreams *cannot* and *will not* be ignored. Many believe that if we try to ignore them, our illnesses or addictions will worsen until we "wake up." Marion Woodman says that "our solution may be to take the time to drop into the unconscious, into the nonrational world (where we will find) the order that may replenish the entropy and chaos of the overinflated rational intellect. As Jung pointed out, that's the source of the healing power."[10]

Next to prayer and meditation, our dream communications are the third greatest tool we have in our search for God, for wholeness, for healing. In our 12-Step programs we continually seek "honesty, open-mindedness, and the willingness to learn," without which we re-create that spiritual void that led to our disorder in the first place. Our dreams will lead us into the void to face our fears and denial and help create our spiritual program—through our 12 Steps. They will be more honest than we could ever ask for: about our progress, our defects of character, our relationships to others.

Our dreams will be more honest than our sponsors, because they know us better. They will be more honest with us than our waking selves even, because they can tap into higher realms than we consciously have access to. Often we are afraid to knowingly delve too deeply for fear that, instead of finding our spiritual selves, *we will lose ourselves.* Just as John Mack, the 1977 Pulitzer Prize-winning biographer of *Lawrence of Arabia,* told *Omni* magazine, "There is a great fear of opening up our world beyond what we know."[11]

But our dreams will bypass this common fear. Our dreams will be open-minded because the shadows of our conscious fears and prejudices will be erased by the Light that will guide us (whether you define that light as God, Shiva, Allah, angles, celestial beings, or simply the Fellowship). We believe our spiritual guides want what's best for us, regardless of how fearful or close-minded we were when we started out. Our dreams will open the doors for all those willing to learn by "stepping over the threshold" into the void at the center of self.

Today, Western society is enjoying a revival of ancient, time-honored spiritual paths, and this revival is being spearheaded by society's flourishing metaphysical and 12-Step programs. Those of us who participate in these programs are gaining back our God-given right to question, pursue, and commune with God and the angels—to seek our Higher Nature and Higher Power with freedom, curiosity, and unprejudiced enthusiasm.

2

Processing Your Dream Messages

Once we decide to pursue the understanding of our dreams and their significance to us, we must first learn the *process* of dreamwork. To understand this process, we can begin by comparing it to the process of working our Steps. We begin 12-Step work by interpreting the Step on which we happen to be working. This interpretation involves finding the *principle* that the Step represents to us. After interpreting it into a principle, we transform that principle into personal significance to our lives. The *act of creating the significance* from the principle, therefore, is the transformation part of the process in which dream messages are *transformed* into usable tools.

In 12-Step programs, we say that individual people have individual programs because, although the Steps read the same for everyone, individuals have their own interpretations of them and their own way of transforming their interpretations into individual meaning. The process looks like this:

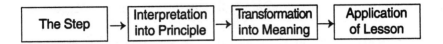

Working Step 5 is a good example of this process. Step 5 reads, "Admitted to God, to ourselves, and to another human being the exact nature of our wrongs." To me, the interpretation of this Step boils down to the principle of honesty. What honesty *means to me* becomes the transformation of the interpretation. This process, from interpretation to application, helps change the old self into a bit of the new self which is striving for wholeness, healing, and spiritual integrity. It is a miraculous metamorphosis.

In 12-Step dreamwork, we practice the same process. Each of us has dream symbols that we interpret in our own way. This leads to an individual understanding of each dream's significance to us. The *act of understanding the significance* becomes our transformation point. We are transforming the interpretation of symbols into a meaningful message. This can result in an insight into our behavior, an understanding of an emotional reaction, or some guidance on future actions that we must take.

Thus, we become the transformer for the messages from our Higher Power, spiritual guides, and our higher self. Without our cooperation first, as an interpreter of symbols, and second, as a transformer of the message content, and finally as the applier of knowledge—our dreams will fall into the meaningless category discussed later in this chapter. Like the process of working the Steps, there are four segments to successful dreamwork. Here is the process:

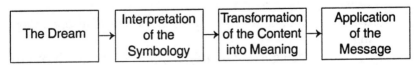

The interpretation and the transformation of the dream images into messages are the most intimidating part of dreamwork because that is when we must be disciplined, knowledgeable, and eventually responsible for the outcome. We can't hand this job over to some professional. It is *our* work. Just as in AA, where no one else can get sober or recover for us, in dreamwork no one else can interpret, transform, and apply the lessons in our lives. However, with a clear understanding of the goal, process, and naturalness of dreamwork, the most reluctant of us will make the very best dreamwork processors.

Dreams and Visions

The first concept to understand in exploring the dream world is that, in terms of interpretability, dreams and visions are almost interchangeable. It is interesting to note that visions are the dreams we have while awake, and dreams come to us in our sleep. They spring from the same source and are often spoken of interchangeably in the Bible (Numbers 12:6, Daniel 2:19, Acts 2:17-18). The "day-dreams" that we call "visions," however, are not to be confused with "daydreaming," which is unfocused wandering, often lost thoughts. Visions are focused, almost trancelike concentrations when definite information is conveyed, accompanied often by intense sounds, sights, and feelings.

In this book we will give dreams and visions equal dominion in our work, and it must be noted that the interpretation and transformation processes follow the same progression. Basically there are four categories of dreams and visions that deal with the various aspects of our lives. These are:

- *Meaningless:* subconscious prattle, internal disturbances, external disturbances
- *Psychic:* past lives, foreshadowings, visionary, dreaming for others, astral traveling, communicating with the dead
- *Guidance:* lessons, problem solving, health and diagnostic, service to others, warnings
- *Reassurance:* congratulatory, praising, supportive, encouraging

The first two categories will not concern us as much in our dreamwork as the second two. *Meaningless* dreams can be caused by noises we've heard outside that disturb our minds and can be interpreted in a dream as a replay of the chain-saw massacre when actually it is our partner snoring. Similarly, if we ate beans for supper and our insides are smoldering, we may experience a nightmare in the form of a complaint from our bodies. Very often, nightmares fall into this category.

Elsie Sechrist in her work, *Dreams: Your Magic Mirror,* reports that nightmares in which one cannot call out or get away are usually caused by the wrong diet and can be cured by a simple change in eating habits. Another reason why dreams can be meaningless is because we don't *think* they have meaning. Like someone who rambles in a monologue with no intent, purpose, or real interest in the conversation, when we refuse to acknowledge that dreams have meaning, they can take on a meaningless, rambling quality. Dream clinicians often say, "Use it or lose it," because when we don't give credence to our dreams, they likewise don't give useful information to us.

Psychic dreams, as fascinating as they are, won't generally concern us in the 12-Step approach to interpretation. Period dreams, complete with costumes and sets, are often glimpses into past lives. Sometimes we will have visionary dreams that give us insight into world events or in which we can communicate with the dead. For example, a few months after my stepmother Ginny had died, I found myself talking to her by the side of my bed.

Ginny had been a vivacious woman in love with life, and she had fought her cancer, the disease that took her, heroically. My stepmother asked how I was. We chatted for a while and suddenly she stopped and looked at me seriously. "I really am dead, aren't I?" I held her hand and whispered, "Yes." Ginny just needed a little extra help in breaking away from the life she had so dearly loved. This dream was not some spiritual revelation that needed interpreting; it was just what it appeared to be—a communication with my departed stepmother.

There are, however, a few *Psychic* dreams we will want to look at in relation to our 12-Step work. Occasionally, predictions of trouble ahead are helpful to us in our program and can strengthen our spiritual resolves before the predicted happy event or negative situation takes place. Everything important that ever occurs in our life is rehearsed first in our dreams. Cayce has said that "any condition ever becoming reality is first dreamed."[1]

A belief in reincarnation can be helpful in discovering how past lives may have contributed to present concerns. I know that the problems between my daughter and me are highly influenced by past lives and less by our addictions in this life. This knowledge has been helpful to me in dealing with her seemingly unwarranted negative emotions. My mother discovered that, lifetime after lifetime, she had been isolated and cut off from people. It is intriguing to see her in this lifetime as an alcoholic, a disease that isolates one from others, and that her only route to recovery from this disease lay in joining groups and in fellowship with others!

Occasionally, dreams are given that contain a message meant for another person who can't receive it for one reason or another. We are meant to share the message or work with that individual in some way as a part of our service to others. I remember once telling my stepdaughter, Tammy, that I'd had two dreams for her real mother. The dreams told me that her mother was ill, but resisted going to the doctor (they were literal dreams—there was no interpretation involved). In a wild attempt to get her attention, her subconscious reality reached out to the only person around her who might be attuned to the other realm, which was I. Although by the time I conveyed the message, Tammy's mother had finally gone to her doctor (and found that she was diabetic), they were both amazed that I could get such information from my dreams. Other than these exceptions, *Psychic* dreams, for the most part, contribute to a different aspect of spiritual growth than what we are exploring with the 12-Step program.

Now we come to the *Guidance* dreams. This is where we will reach across into another realm and gain access to all the authority we care to petition for advancing in our programs. *Guidance* dreams are where our higher self, our spiritual guides, or even the Divine Presence itself speaks to us, teaches us, offers suggestions, reveals our shortcomings, warns us, chides us, etc. Tremendous benefits have been accorded humankind during the realities of sleep. It has been reported that Albert Einstein found some important solutions to equations during his sleep; part of the last movement of Handel's *Messiah* came from a dream; Benjamin Franklin found many of his inventive ideas in dreams; the poem *Kubla Khan* by Samuel Taylor Coleridge was revealed to him in a dream.

In the book, *Dreams and Spiritual Growth*, the authors tell us that "dreams are reservoirs of psychological and spiritual energies."[2] But we might add "physical energies," too. Our *Guidance* dreams not only access the mind and spirit, but the body as well. We say in our 12-Step programs that our ailments are threefold: of the mind and spirit as well as of the body. Accordingly, we find that our dreams will aid us in health and diagnoses, too.

My mother belonged to an Edgar Cayce study group in 1985 that concentrated its work on dreams. One man in the group had a dream that simply told him to drink Uva Ursi tea. Although he discussed it with the group, he did not heed the warning and two years later found that he had bladder cancer. This particular tea is known for its cancer-fighting properties. We'll never know if, by drinking the tea, he would have had a different outcome with the cancer, but it is prudent to remember that our dreams are meant to serve us, not scare us.

I recently had a dream which told me to gather, can, and eat cranberries—lots! After several months of eating them, I stopped, thinking enough time had elapsed. Not too long afterward, while I was in Russia, a young Asian girl gave me an unusual gift for no apparent reason—a jar of cranberries that she had picked and canned herself! I took this as a direct reminder from my guides and immediately began eating cranberries again. So far, I seem perfectly healthy. I may never know what illness or illnesses I have averted, if any—but for me it isn't worth taking a chance on ignoring my dreams.

Once we validate and implement our dreams, then we will begin to receive the pure pleasure side of the exchange, whereby our higher self, spiritual guides, or the Divine Presence will say, "Hey, you're doing a good job!" *Reassurance* dreams will congratulate us for a lesson well learned, a task accomplished, or simply offer words of encouragement for us to keep on trying.

Long ago, when I had broken up with my fiancé after he had a slip in AA for the fourth time, I knew it was hopeless to plan a future with him. In addition to the broken plans and broken commitments to a sober spiritual life together, I was also losing a measure of financial security (he was a pilot) that he had offered at the time. One day after talking with him briefly, I broke down crying for all that was lost. Suddenly, a powerful vision appeared to me: I was flying in a plane like his, only his was on the ground while I soared above. A deep feeling of love, completeness, and abundance enveloped me. Immediately I recognized the support and encouragement offered by my spiritual guides. They were telling me that while my fiancé was left behind (on the ground), I would rise to greater spiritual heights without him (my flying alone) and have financial security equal to or greater than what he could offer (I was in *my own plane* above him).

The reassurance that all was well was very comforting to me then and also proved to be more than accurate as the future unfolded. The last time I saw him, he was sitting drunk in a house in Denver, having lost his plane, his job, and most of his friends while I have moved ever forward and sit today writing this book, in love with life and on fire with a passion to bolster the message of the 12-Step programs around the world. The comfort, encouragement, and joy offered through dreams and visions is an indubitable legacy of the quest for spirituality in all of us.

Interpreting Your Life Like a Dream

There is a new technique in vogue today that is being used by people who are already familiar with interpreting and transforming dreams. It is the process of ascribing meaning to given events that occur in one's life—to process the events as if they were dreams. Indeed, many people consider life to be little more than a dream—fleeting and ever illusionary. "The dream is dreaming itself" is a saying used by the Kalahari Bushmen and reflects the sense contained in the popular song *Row, Row, Row Your Boat:* "Life is but a dream." Of course, the idea that life is illusionary and dreamlike is not a new one. What *is* new is the idea of interpreting life as though it were a dream.

A retired psychotherapist and prolific contemporary writer, Dr. Glenn Williston, consults with clients on unique personal growth tools, one of which is interpreting life events. He believes that the incidents and situations in our lives are full of significance and that happenings can "talk" to us, if we would only listen. Dr. Williston points out to his clients that understanding or interpreting our life can explain why seemingly negative things happen to people who practice spiritual principles and why others enjoy endless runs of "good" luck for no apparent worthy reason.

Again, we become the interpreters and transformers in this technique. Processing life events, like dreamwork processing, has four segments:

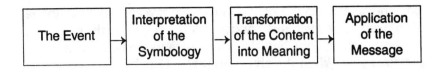

Dr. Williston presented a good example for this process in an interview by journalist Daniel Rosen.[3] A client of his was experiencing a series of frustrating and elusive electrical problems in her home. Dr. Williston helped her to see the comparison between the wiring of her home and the wiring of her body (i.e., neurotransmitters). He referred her to a neurobiologist, who diagnosed her with RADD (Residual Attention Deficit Disorder). This "resulted in our effective treatment that literally and figuratively lit up her life." It is even more interesting to note that electricians could not find the source of the problem in her house, but the wiring problem cleared up without explanation once she began the RADD therapy!

Basically, Dr. Williston talks about three different categories of meaningful experience: true dreams (including nightmares), personal daily events (including the crises that he labels "daymares"), and fantasies or daydreams. They are really all the same in terms of purpose and interpretation: they all alert us to seeing something we are reluctant to see. They urge us to do something we should be doing or implore us to stop doing something that is hurting us or others.

Robea, my personal psychic, also uses life-events interpretation in her psychic therapeutic work. She described how she uses this technique in her own life: "I received five speeding tickets, a severe blow to the right side of my head, and a scratch on my right cornea all within a three-year period. At the time I was living with a man, Clay, who I thought was my soul mate," she said. He was abusing drugs and alcohol, but Robea didn't want to see it. His drug abuse eventually led to his molesting her daughter. If she had been paying attention to interpreting her life events, Robea believes she could have prevented the outcome.

"The car that I received the five tickets in," she continued, "was the one Clay had picked out for me. It was also red." The tickets were warning her (red car) that she shouldn't be speeding along his life path (he picked the car). The left side of the body represents the female and the right side represents the male. The blow to the right side and scratch on the right cornea were revealing in that Robea didn't want to be *aware* of Clay's true nature and to *see* the situation.

Her daughter, Sara, had also hurt her tailbone two times in the previous year. When the abuse occurred, Clay had lain on top of Sara's back and rubbed against her tailbone. So even her daughter's life events were signaling Robea!

"I was so timid," my psychic explained to me, "that with Clay's repeated begging and promises of deep spiritual change, I continued to allow him to live with us, even after turning him in. But, thank God, by this time, I was paying attention." Then she hit a doe smack in the center of her blue car and broke both the doe's hind legs. In Indian lore, a doe represents the gentleness that meets the monster on the way to heaven and melts his heart because she is unafraid. This was telling Robea not to be afraid to face the truth (blue car) and that this man broke their trust and she must break off the relationship and leave it behind. "The monster was my fear of being alone, but I was able to get past it and break it off before the universe got deadly serious with me," she concluded.

I thought Robea's story was fascinating, but didn't actually give it much overall credence. Even though I have often uttered to myself, "Life is but a dream," and wondered which was more real, dreamtime or lifetime, it wasn't until a recent occurrence in my own life that I considered interpreting life like a dream as a viable method of personal growth.

I have never received a moving violation since I began driving twenty-seven years ago, until last fall when I received *three* in one week! One was for speeding, one was for not signaling before changing lanes, and the other was for making an illegal left-hand turn. I was furious with the officers, with the stupid laws, and most of all with myself. Normally I am the type of law-abiding driver that stops at a stop sign in the middle of the desert with no cars in sight for fifty miles. What happened?

I phoned Robea, complaining bitterly, and she told me to interpret the experiences as if they were dreams. Robea repeated the above example from her own life. I thought it was all very amusing, but rather wanted her to tell me what *outside* force was manipulating my life. She hadn't been much help, I thought.

Then a few months later, I had a dream. I was explaining to someone that a ticket was my wake-up call to pay attention on the road.

I told that to the judge, too. My dream was warning me to wake up to the messages presented in my life! It was also telling me to pay attention to Robea. The speeding ticket was warning me to slow down, the not-signaling ticket was "signaling" me to watch out on the road, and the illegal-turn citation was warning me not to turn from my true path by disregarding my mission of teaching people to interpret—in this case, interpreting life events!

Although not everyone will be comfortable viewing events in life as messages for learning and growing, it is a way for us to step out of the role of "victim" (look what some person, place, or thing is doing to me) and transform it into victory (look how I've improved myself as a result of this). Our 12-Step programs are based on personal responsibility; using life events, addictions, and tragedies to learn and grow makes us ever more the victors, not the victims.

Levels of Consciousness

For the purposes of insight and learning, then, we human beings can gather information and accept guidance (from dreams, visions, and life events) to be brought back to our conscious reality for application in our everyday lives. During dreamtime, our conscious mind is put aside and our subconscious or higher conscious is free to tap sources from other realms. Edgar Cayce described a higher level of knowledge and help wherein lay the universal mind and personal God,[4] while Carl Jung, a psychiatrist and dream specialist, referred to the collective unconscious.

Before we look further into how we process dreams, visions, and life events, it is crucial to understand the terminology that we are using when speaking of the unconscious, higher conscious, subconscious, collective unconscious, superconscious, and universal mind. This is important because by using them together, we are combining disciplines whose terms are not always interchangeable. For our purposes, I am creating artificial groupings based on common-sense definitions and from the generally accepted hierarchy of spiritual sagacity:

1. *Conscious:* This is the waking state. It embodies what we know, think we know, and are aware of. We think with the conscious mind on the earth as we deal with the circumstances of the physical plane.

2. *Unconscious:* This is the portion of the mind which operates on the earth plane to keep the body going, such as heart beat, breathing, digestion. It holds all the memories and influences from our bodies and minds since our conception, but has no real ability to think other than on an elementary survival basis. It operates instinctively, more like a computer, using input and output with no discernment whatsoever. Our conscious minds generally don't know what is going on in the unconscious.

3. *Subconscious or higher conscious:* The dictionary gives *subconscious* the same definition as *unconscious,* but we will use the definition of Cayce's who once said that the subconscious mind is the conscious mind of the soul. This would also be considered the mind of our higher self and is the receiver of dreams and visions. Our subconscious communicates with our earthly conscious and is the sieve which screens communications from other realms.

4. *Superconscious, collective unconscious, or universal mind:* This is the consciousness that contains all knowledge, contains the akashic record, and is the source of divine communications. Some religious authorities teach that there is a myriad of levels for the superconscious. They sometimes consider the superconscious to be another dimension of levels where the attainment of each will advance us toward the Godhead. The superconscious preeminently is a state or dimension not generally available to our waking self. It is the source of dream guidance; spiritual guides; the still, small voice—basically the source of all that is.

On the other hand, the more scientifically minded like to think not of a superconscious, but of a collective unconscious that is not divine at all, but simply an hereditary memory held in the DNA of the race. For simplicity's sake, we will define the collective unconscious of Jung and the superconscious as the same well from which we all drink of the spirit, the source of all that is—the universal mind. These definitions, when used consistently in our dreamwork, will help dispel undue confusion over terms.

Symbology

From the universal mind or the collective unconscious springs an alternate language, the language of symbology. In our dreams, this language usually presents messages in terms of symbols, rather than stating them in what we'd term an obvious manner. Before we delve into the language of symbology and how to transform that symbology for everyday use, let us first examine the obvious ways in which dreams speak to us.

Sometimes our dreams and visions speak to us literally, like in my communication with Ginny. Another example of a literal dream, one I had a few months ago, involved a rap song which erupted with "God is serving you right." This was particularly grating to me because I dislike rap music. I had, prior to that, been petitioning God for several things in my life, and I wasn't getting what I thought I needed and/or wanted. The dream was literally telling me that although it may not be in the form I fancied, God was doing for me *just exactly* what was needed—God *was* serving me right.

Most often though, the messages of our dreams come to us in a symbolic form, such as parables, metaphors, allegories, and analogies. We will begin our task of learning to clarify the content by first examining symbols and correctly assessing their meaning. This will be covered in the section "Your Dream Glossary" below. In the section "From Symbol Interpretation to Content Transformation" (p. 33), we will address how to transform the stories they create into meaningful life lessons that you can use. Finally, in chapter 3 we will discuss how to use the process of dreamwork with the 12-Step programs. But it is important to have a base of knowledge in general dream processing before you advance to 12-Step dream processing. So we will begin by learning how to build your own glossary.

Your Dream Glossary

Carl Jung believed that the dreamer is the one best qualified to discern what a dream means. The dreamer, or we can say "processor," is the only one who can refashion the metaphors into meaningful messages applicable to his or her own life. Jung believed not only in the collective unconscious with its many universal symbols that apply to all humankind, but he asserted that the personal history of each processor determines the ultimate meaning of each dream. In fact, every respected dreamwork professional whom I've ever studied—from Jung to Sechrist, Woodman, Robea, and Cayce—all agree that the processor him/herself has the final word on every interpretation. Therefore, rather than rely solely on the dictionaries or glossaries of dream symbols written by other people, your first task is to create a dream glossary of your own. This personal dreamwork glossary will be unique to each one.

In Part II you will find "Your Dreamwork Glossary." It is a convenient format in which you will record your dream symbols and the special meaning each one holds for you, so that you can refer to them later as you process future dreams. This will enable you to build a personalized reference guide to your own dream world.

The format of the dreamwork glossary divides dream symbols into broad categories that make them easier to record and interpret. This format is loosely derived from the categories used by Elsie Sechrist in *Dreams: Your Magic Mirror* because it is easier to understand and clarify the images when they are grouped in like associations. When you have a dream and begin to process it, you will then enter each image according to the following categories:

The Four Elements (Earth, Water, Air, and Fire)
Colors
Numbers
Animate Objects (Domestic and Wild Animals, Birds, Marine Life, and Insects)
Behavior and Activity (Includes Sexual Dreams)
Clothes, Accessories, and Jewelry
Figures and Features
Plants
Health, Illness, and Death
Inanimate Objects (All "Things" Not Listed Elsewhere)
Spiritual Symbols
Vehicles and Buildings

Each image that you eventually record in each category will have three relevant levels of definition for you to consider. These levels will aid you in discovering the meaning of the symbols. They are:

Universal Meaning, which embodies and teaches certain basic truths that apply to most of humankind (some universal definitions will be provided for you in the discussion section of each category);

Cultural Meaning, which embodies tradition and history, that provide lessons and meanings for people born into that culture (cultural definitions will be discussed in a general way in the introductory text of each category along with the basis for the universal meanings);

Personal Significance, which comes from you and is based on your subjective life experiences.

Take a moment and read pages 75-78 in "Your Dreamwork Glossary" in Part II. Then skim through the remainder and acquaint yourself with the format you will be using. We will introduce you to each category with a brief explanation of the basis for defining the universal meaning of the images that will be found in that grouping. This introductory text is a broad outline of attributes and qualities humankind generally ascribes to the creatures, objects, or conditions we find in that category. It will help give you a rationale for establishing the specific cultural and personal definitions that you will list in the blank format provided.

Following the brief introductory text will be a list of related idioms and sayings that Western society commonly uses. Familiarizing yourself with these sayings will impart a sense of how the subconscious may choose to "play on words" when communicating with you, the dreamer.

Next, you will find a list of words that fits into that grouping. The generally accepted universal meaning of the word is provided. These universal definitions are not necessarily what you will write down as you build your dream glossary, although they may be.

Finally, you will see your blank glossary format. This is where you will record the images that come to you in your dreams. Notice that the blank line beside where you record your image is divided into two sections—"Cultural Meaning" and "Personal Significance."

Once you write a dream image in your glossary, try to think of how the culture you most closely identify with defines that image, and then record that definition. The culture you identify with can be as general as "Western," "North American," "Judeo-Christian," or as specific as "Gay," "Corporate," or "Feminist." This will depend on your current viewpoint and the content and context of the dream. Don't let the multifarious nature of the word "culture" throw you. Actually, what you surmise that other people think the symbol or symbolic behavior means will be the correct cultural meaning for you. Your mind will naturally fall into the cultural context appropriate to you. Trust me.

Next, find your individual interpretation to record. This may be the same as the universal or cultural meaning or it may be entirely different. The main distinction between "cultural" and "personal" is that the cultural meaning is what a *whole class of people think* the symbol means, while your personal significance is *what you think* it means.

You are not meant to fill in your glossary immediately, but slowly as your dreams are presented to you from the other realm. Upon awakening, record your dreams in a diary that you keep just for this purpose. Later, identify the symbols that your subconscious and superconscious provided in the dream and record them one by one in your glossary. You will want to list new symbols with each dream you remember, only omitting entries as they start repeating themselves. This process will enlarge your glossary for future reference. Soon you will be intimately familiar with the language your subconscious uses with you, and you will possess the most accurate dreamwork glossary in the world—for you!

Here's an example that illustrates how to use "Your Dreamwork Glossary." A friend of mine, Clara, had a dream in which her brother (who was married to her best friend but having an affair) walked into her house carrying a huge dead fish. The young woman with whom he was having the affair was carrying the tail of this huge fish. They set it down, and Clara cut out some sections which were pink, fried them, then she and her best friend ate it while her brother and lover refused. Since this particular dream was referring to a real situation, the affair, each of the people represented themselves and would not have to be interpreted symbolically. However, we are dealing with several symbols (the dead fish and the color pink) and several symbolic activities (carrying in a dead fish, preparing a meal, and eating a meal). In Clara's glossary, she would list under *Animate Objects* "dead fish."

Clara knows that in our Christian culture a fish is a symbol for Christ, so for her a dead fish means "dead to Christ." This is what her brother's affair represented to her. My friend loves to prepare and serve food, so on a personal level this fish would mean "nourishment" to her. Clara's glossary under *Animate Objects* would look like this:

ANIMATE OBJECTS

Symbol	Cultural Meaning	Personal Significance
Fish	Christ/Christ Consciousness	Spiritual Nourishment

The universal interpretation of the color "pink" is generally "love," and since Clara attaches no other particular personal significance to the color "pink" (i.e., it's neither her favorite color nor does she hate it or associate it only with babies), then the word "pink" would be listed under *Colors* as:

COLORS

Symbol	Cultural Meaning	Personal Significance
Pink	Love	Love

Clara is known as the strength of her family and the advice-giver. Her brother approaching her house, then, would mean that he is seeking her counsel. The actions in this dream, listed under *Behavior*, might look like this in her glossary:

BEHAVIOR

Symbol	Cultural Meaning	Personal Significance
Carrying Dead Fish	Dead to Christ	Heavy Burden
Preparing Food	Nourishing Others	Giving Advice
Eating	Accepting Nourishment	Accepting Advice

Thus, her brother's affair is a heavy burden to him from which he seeks the advice of his sister. His actions show that, to her, he is dead to Christ. His sister tries to counsel him with the love of Christ and Christian principles (eat of my flesh), but only her friend eats (accepts the advice in the form of the love of Christ) and the adulterous couple refuse. This dream is showing Clara that although her brother comes to her for advice, he is refusing to listen, and the only ones she can really help will be her best friend and herself. It is also amusing to note the double entendre of the mistress carrying a little "tail" in this dream.

By writing her symbols down in this way, Clara will be able to consult her glossary in the future for her personal spiritual symbolic language. In future dreams she will know that a fish, for her, is one of the symbols for Christ. Clara will know that when she prepares and serves meals, she is offering to nourish people spiritually through advice, and so on.

With each dream, you will be adding symbols and symbolic behavior until you notice that you already have a particular symbol recorded, and the meaning of the symbols will start to become strikingly clear the instant you remember them. For instance, although dogs are universally friends and helpmates to humankind and known as "man's best friend" in the American culture, I have a personal fear of big dogs. So in my dreams, big dogs always represent a fear of some sort. Sometimes, taken in the cultural context, they represent my fear of friends trying to help me (loss of independence). However, I have a Pomeranian whom I adore and go to great lengths to take care of. My glossary under *Animate Objects* looks like this:

ANIMATE OBJECTS

Symbol	Cultural Meaning	Personal Significance
Dogs	Man's Best Friend	Deep Fear
Little Dogs	Cuddly Companions	Friendships to Be Protected

Remember that in different cultures the emphasis will be different, because, although the universal meaning of dogs is to serve humanity, *in what capacity* they serve is a cultural bias. They can "serve" a friend; they can "serve" as a working animal; they can "serve" as a meal. In America we are likely to see a little dog as a companion, while in some Asian countries the dog may be seen as a main course—both of these ideas still contain the concept of service to humankind!

In Russia, symbolic actions in dreams are often taken to mean the opposite of what you are seeing. If you dream of sickness, for example, Russians believe that you will enjoy health; and if you dream of war, there will be peace. They see the dream world as a sort of balancing mechanism for real life.

Even the Russian Orthodox cross symbolizes this polarizing attitude. It is constructed with a second bar underneath the first that slants—pointing to heaven above or hell below, your choice. At the same time their churches are extremely demanding, requiring strict adherence to dogma. The priests exact a huge price from their congregations, illustrated simply by the rule against sitting down in church even when services last all night. The universal meaning of the cross is balance in all directions, but the dream glossary of a Russian may look like this:

SPIRITUAL SYMBOLS

Symbol	Cultural Meaning	Personal Significance
Cross	Choice of Heaven or Hell	Suffer in Church

While the dream glossary of an American might look like this:

SPIRITUAL SYMBOLS

Symbol	Cultural Meaning	Personal Significance
Cross	Longsuffering, Vampire Protection	Love of Christ

You may want to use one or more dream symbol reference books, such as *Dreams: Your Magic Mirror* by Elsie Sechrist, *The Dream Book* by Betty Bethards, *The Dream Dictionary* by Jo Jean Boushahla and Virginia Reidel-Geubtner, or Native American-influenced symbols such as the Medicine Cards (see Bibliography), or any of a dozen good titles to help you get started—although this step isn't actually necessary. The most important dream dictionary you will ever own is the one you create in this book. You will also want to use the index, which lists many dream symbols you might deal with and shows you how the people who contributed dreams to this book found their own meanings.

Quick Techniques for Finding
Individual Dream Symbol Meanings

Occasionally, the meanings of symbols are not readily apparent to the dreamer for one reason or another. There are many books listed in the Bibliography that contain additional techniques and also dream exercises that you may find beneficial. But to me, the few simple and quick practices listed below are all that I or my dream consultees ever need for finding individual dream symbol meanings.

1. *Word Association:* Pretend you have a dream in which you are wearing a nightgown. You know that the nightgown is significant, but can't quite grasp the meaning. Get a pencil and paper and write "nightgown"; beside it write the first word or words, *no matter how silly,* that come to you. It might be "legs." Then write "nightgown" again and repeat the association. The second words might be "not see-through." A third try might bring "cover"; you would begin to see that a nightgown to you means "something to cover the legs that is not see-through," thus meaning "modesty."

Another person might get the association of "breasts," "sexy," and "strut" which, depending upon the person, might clearly mean "sexual availability." Most likely a nightgown will have something to do with the bedroom and sex in the universal context. But if you were forced at one time to wear a nightgown to school because your grandmother insisted it looked enough like a dress and this action humiliated and traumatized you, then a nightgown to you could represent humiliation. This association exercise is an easy and very effective tool for understanding the unique symbology of your dreams.

2. *Asking:* In this simple exercise, you relax into a meditative state and simply picture your higher self or a "wise dream interpreter"— maybe Elsie Sechrist, Edgar Cayce, or someone of your own mystical creation—then ask, "What does the symbol 'race car' mean to me?" Listen quietly to the response from your "wise dream interpreter." The answer will be correct because it is *your subconscious* talking to you.

For instance, I used to consciously associate the color "black" with evil and death. It drove me wild that priests and nuns wore this color when they were supposed to be so holy. So I went into a meditative state and asked why they wore black and what it meant. A Chinese man, dressed in a black robe, majestically descended from the sky and chuckled amicably at me. "Black is not a color, but the *absence* of color," the holy man grinned. "Therefore, black is the most *humble* noncolor to wear." So even though the universal symbology of black is the unconscious, what is past and hidden, while our cultural connotations are evil and death, my personal meaning will be a combination of the above and, depending upon the context, humbleness!

From Symbol Interpretation to Content Transformation

In the long run, it isn't so much the symbols of dreaming that confound us. After all, we think in symbols. If someone mentions a circus bear, we picture a bear in the ring. We don't see the word *bear* in our mind. If we hear the word *blue*, we picture the color, not spell the word out mentally. So symbology, by itself, is not difficult. What confounds most people is when the dream is presented like a riddle to be solved. Unlike the pictographs we drew as children where an eye, a heart, and a "U" meant "I love you," our dream symbols don't spell out the communication so clearly—leaving us instead to "solve" some cryptic message.

There are a number of answers to this problematic language of the night. Some people simply say, "Dream symbols are the language of the soul," as if no other explanation is needed. In *The Dream Book*, Betty Bethards explains that her guidance says, "Dreams are given symbolically because once you know your own symbols you cannot mistake the message."[5] In *Dreams and Spiritual Growth*, the authors mention Jesus' controversial—and I might add cryptic in itself—answer to why He spoke in parables as "(I speak) to them in parables: because they seeing see not; and hearing they hear not, neither do they understand." (Matthew 13:13) The authors think this might be a clue as to why we dream in parables. "He that hath ears to hear, let him hear." (Luke 8:8)[6]

Some people get very technical and talk about the left brain/right brain issues. They explain that the right brain—our spiritual, symbolic side—knows very few words and that most of the dreaming must occur there because many of our dreams are in symbols similar to the thinking patterns of the right brain. It is the logical left brain that uses words; thus, dreams and visions come to us in their own language from the nonverbal right side.

Psychologists often speak of defense mechanisms that we use in dreaming to protect us from perceived dangers in the world. They say that dreaming in analogies and metaphors are more productive than literal presentations of our fears, traumas, and problems because it is so hard to broach terrifying subjects head on. Their explanation is that our dreams work with our problems in a psychological "beat around the bush" sort of way, shielding us from the truth until we can face it squarely.

One of the most viable explanations of dream language is Jungian in origin. According to this theory, the dream metaphor or image works on all the senses (soma) simultaneously. It works on your imagination, your emotional body, your intellect, sight, memories, and education. A dream presents you with one image that is meaningful to *all* aspects of your being, instantaneously. This can produce a "eureka" type of recognition and is more powerful—more transforming, if you will—to your whole self.

The truth is, probably none of us really knows for sure why some dreams are literal, some symbolic, and some half and half. What we do know for sure is that when dreams and visions are transformed by us to meaningful messages, they will bring us closer to God so long as we apply the homilies presented on a daily basis. Although the way in which professionals versus laypeople choose to perceive these homilies can be a matter of contention at best, or psychiatric diagnosis at worst, we continue (as a society) to move ahead in using them.

In shifting from the interpretation of specific symbols to understanding the entire meaning of each dream, Betty Bethards explains the beginning steps as these: "First they [the dream settings] give the time reference for the problem, situation, or program you are running. For example, if you are shown a house you lived in when you were a child, the house represents an old program or awareness of self that started way back then.

"Second, they [dreams] will show you how the problem is manifesting now in your life and present awareness—what is surrounding it.

"Third, they will present the solution to the situation, or how to learn from and move beyond the program or problem that is limiting you."[7]

Most *Guidance* dreams will follow this general course. So after you have identified your personal meanings for each of the symbols or symbolic actions in your dreams, visions, or life events, you look in the dream for the time frame where the seeds of the problem began, then check the dream surroundings and actions for how the issue is making itself felt now. Finally, the solution or conclusion will be presented as the last segment of the dream (if you remember the whole dream).

Quick Techniques for Finding the Theme of Your Dream

Again, there are a number of very fine books that will give you numerous exercises and drills to get at meanings, but the process is generally pretty simple. Look first for a purely literal meaning. Failing that:

1. Decipher the meaning of each symbol and symbolic action
2. Find your time frame so that you know where the problem began
3. Determine the present manifestation of the problem
4. Discover the solution

If you find that the theme just keeps eluding you and you feel it definitely has significance and cannot be tossed into the *Meaningless* category, then you can try these simple techniques:

1. *Sentence completion:* Write down, "This dream is mainly dealing with my _____." It is very important that you put the first thing that comes to you—don't edit! Do this three or four times and the meaning should pop out like the cork from a champagne bottle.

2. *Written or spoken dialogue:* Relax yourself and slip into a meditative state; create an imaginative picture of your wise dream interpreter (as in the *Asking* drill, p. 32). Then either mentally or by writing down the question, ask what significance this dream message carries for you. Your interpreter or the dream figures that you

talk to will answer sincerely if you ask sincerely. This is not automatic writing in which "spirits" write through you. It is a dialogue with your subconscious—the consciousness of your soul that knows the content and intent of your dreams. The character's purpose should quickly be revealed to you. To help illustrate, my friend's brother, David, had this dream:

> I was riding my bicycle and both my sons were with me. Then we tumbled into the water. My sons sank and one came up. I asked him where the youngest was. "He's at the bottom sleeping," my son answered. I dove down to bring the youngest up and he was fine.

David woke up and decided to have a dream dialogue with his "sons." His youngest son said that he needed to sleep to be safe. He told David, "I'm not your son. I'm you at this age." To protect himself from the abuse he suffered at that age, David had put his "child" to sleep. David recognized that he never did play or have fun as an adult—that side of him had been put to sleep. This experience helped David to recognize the problem his psyche was dealing with and he was able to take corrective measures to help his "child" surface from emotions once again.

Remember that even though we get much of our spiritual guidance through dreams in a sort of parable or riddle, this is not meant to drive us away from this source of help. Dream symbols have been the language of the soul since humans appeared on earth and are prevalent from our early sacred beliefs in all major religions, in our world's mythologies, and even in the fairy tales that we use to teach our children. This symbology is a rich language from the soul that requires only interest and self-discipline to master.

In the processing of dreams, visions, and life events, we will use the interpretation of the symbols and then transform the message into meaning for our daily lives. Neither the interpretation nor transformation process has to be confusing if we remain open and practice the techniques herein. Once we finish the dreamwork process by applying the lessons presented to us, a true metamorphosis can take place, not unlike the grounded caterpillar who transforms into a free-flying and beautiful butterfly.

3

Dreamwork and
12-Step Enhancement

Even if you're a longtime 12-Step veteran—AA, NA, OA, GA, CA, SA, Coda, or any of the Anon companions—you can probe further into your spiritual lessons by learning more about processing the metaphors in your life. You will be able to fine-tune, attune, and atone your metamorphosed self with the aid and application of your dreams by correlating them directly with the 12 Steps.

If you thought working the 12 Steps without dreams was a great adventure in personal exploration, then you will be astounded at the orbit of this new adventure you are about to embark on. You will learn things about yourself you never thought possible and reach spiritual horizons often only afforded the most ardent devotees in the search for God. I'm not talking about spiritual highs or pink clouds (although certainly that will be a part of this). I am referring to the enhancement of each Step as we apply it in our everyday lives—honesty, more revealing than your bathroom mirror. I'm talking about trust and faith that will nurture you in the worst of life circumstances, moral responsibility that will set your whole existence in order, and service to others that will end up strengthening yourself more than those you aid.

It is also prudent to point out that you probably have not picked this book up by chance. As we say in the fellowships, "You didn't get here by accident," and it is a tenet of universal law as expressed by Edgar Cayce, "For, no soul enters any experience perchance. For it comes with a purpose. And the entity as well as every entity should know: The Divine, the First Cause, is mindful of the entity."[1] So now that we understand that you are *supposed* to be investigating this avenue of 12-Step acceleration, this book should give you the initiative to apply the methods we are about to discuss.

"But I don't dream," you might protest. What you mean to say is, "I don't *remember* my dreams." Scientists have proven that *everyone*—with the possible exception of practicing drunks and junkies—dreams every night. Research from such prestigious institutions as Stanford and Duke tell us that we dream during REM (Rapid Eye Movement) sleep, which occurs with everyone many times during each sleep cycle. Learning to remember our dreams is not at all difficult. In fact, it's as easy as telling ourselves, "I will remember my dreams tonight," just before retiring. (The complete method is discussed in this chapter under *Setup*, p. 49.)

Should any of us still believe we have no dreams or visions of any consequence to process in relation to the 12 Steps, then we can go directly to interpreting and transforming our life events *as if they are dreams*. Processing life events does work. It is just preferable to begin with the dreams so that we don't have to experience traumas on the waking side of reality in order to grow. It is more preferable to dream about getting a speeding ticket and interpret the dream than to *get* the ticket. It is preferable to see our roof on fire in a dream, rather than experience the real thing. It seems apparent that situations present themselves to us in order to bring messages and lessons for recovery and spiritual growth. When we need to learn something, it first appears in a sublime manner, like an intuitive thought. However, the "message" we need increases in intensity and drama, even to crisis proportions, until we "get it." Our spiritual guidance might go through these phases, trying to reach our waking awareness:

Intuition: intuitive thoughts; the still, small voice; sixth sense

Dreams: guidance while sleeping

Visions: manifested guidance while awake

Life events, external: situations with our environment, like houses, cars, jobs

Life events, internal: situations with our bodies, like illnesses, stress, and accidents to self

Tragedies: fatal or chronic illnesses, destroyed relationships, breakdowns, imprisonment

Learning to pay attention at the start of the spiritual communication process has its advantages, which is some measure of serenity. This is not to say that if we pay attention, nothing "bad" will happen to us. Life happens anyway. But if we are listening to our spiritual guidance, we will be in tune with the universe and in the flow of our life. All events, then (whether serious or not), will seem natural, and we will handle them with ease and with grace.

We must also remember that our spiritual guidance isn't always warning or teaching us in a so-called negative sense. We also must listen to the love, humor, generosity, and fulfillment that flows through these phases. We can interpret dreams, visions, and life events that are funny, beautiful, pleasant, enriching, and endearing. We don't seek to find just the "bad" karma to learn from—but recognize that everything, life itself, is our lesson. So whether we choose to call it karma, dharma, fate, or destiny, we know that our spiritual guidance, in whatever form, holds our best interests and happiness always to the forefront.

The Spirituality of Dreamwork

Oftentimes people worry that their dreams are not spiritual enough or spiritually oriented enough. Our dreams do come to us in many different forms and deal with a myriad of situations. But people on planet earth eventually come to understand that we are here to grow spiritually. Our whole existence must lead us back to God. So when we question dreamwork as mundane or superficial, are we forgetting that to better ourselves in any area is to better ourselves spiritually? As it says in the "Big Book," "We try to put spiritual principles to work in every department of our lives. When we do that, we find it solves our problems, too."[2]

Many dream clinicians run across this sort of "prejudice" with their clients. Clients may believe that their dreams, visions, and life events are not holy or hallowed enough to warrant merit. Dream expert Gayle Delaney, in her article "The Spiritual Dimension of Dreams,"[3] shares her thoughts about dream prejudices.

"The other day," she wrote, "a new member of one of our small dream study groups worked on a dream that turned out to be an insightful description and analysis of the troubles she was having with her fiancé. The five practicing dream interviewers were quite pleased with the process and outcome of the dream interview, as was I. Then to our surprise the dreamer looked embarrassed and apologized for having presented such a mundane dream: 'I had hoped this dream would be about my spiritual path, but it's only about my boyfriend. I'm sorry I couldn't have brought in a better dream.' The other group members (who had been in the group for one or two years) tried to reassure the dreamer that some of them had begun dreamwork with similar prejudices and that they had discovered over time that dreams usually deal with our spiritual concerns as the concerns manifest themselves in our relationships with others and in our work."

We are physical, mental/emotional, and spiritual beings. Any one area affects the others. We are one. As Cayce says—"*One*—One—One—*ONE;* Oneness of God, oneness of man's relation, oneness of force, oneness of time, oneness of purpose, *oneness* in every effort—Oneness—Oneness!"[4] So *any* dream that works on our betterment in any area of our lives is considered a spiritual dream! And Cayce also said, "Let them all be sacred, treat [dreams and visions] so . . . "[5]

The Purpose of 12-Step Dreamwork

Once we realize that our sleeping reality is meant to help us grow and that it is sacred, we find that we have a responsibility to get to the dream's purpose and apply it in our lives. We are meant to become the best conceivable beings possible within our scope here on earth. Psychologists and psychiatrists say we need to move toward personal wholeness and unity. Jung called this process "individuation" and Abraham Maslow, who was a respected psychiatrist and innovative spirituality researcher, called this process "self-actualization." Members of 12-Step programs simply call the process "recovery." Whether we label our striving for wholeness with terms like "individuation," "self-actualization," or we simply say "recovery," we are working for the same goal—wholeness of body, mind, and spirit.

What is accomplished by working these Steps is the integration of body, mind, and spirit. Making our dreams part of our program assists us in working the Steps better. They help to provide a link to our Higher Power. This link connects our everyday life to our spiritual awareness, which leads us, in essence, to individuation, self-actualization—i.e., recovery. This link is the sixth sense. Once we develop it, the sixth sense is the single greatest mechanism we can utilize in managing our lives. The "Big Book" states:

> Much has already been said about receiving strength, inspiration, and direction from Him who has all knowledge and power. If we have carefully followed directions, we have begun to sense the flow of His Spirit into us. To some extent we have become God-conscious. We have begun to develop this vital sixth sense.[6]

Regarding the sixth sense, the Cayce readings corroborate with the following passage:

> [The sixth sense] goes *out* into that realm of experience in the relationships of all experiences of that entity that may have been throughout the *eons* of time, or in correlating *with* that as it, that entity, *has* accepted as its criterion or standard of judgments ... within its sphere of activity. Hence ... there may have come that peace, that understanding, that is accorded ... in sleep ... Hence we see how that the action through such sleep, or such quieting as to enter the silence—What do we mean by entering the silence? Entering the presence of that which *is* the criterion of the selves of an entity![7]

Developing this sixth sense (this link to God) is a part of living the more spiritual life we seek. And practicing the principles found in the Steps, aided by prayer, meditation, and dreams, is the clearest path to developing this "vital" sixth sense.

Even so, while some people know the purpose of prayer, meditation, and dreams in their lives, they sometimes fail to recognize the fruits of their labor. After an address I gave at the Betty Ford Center, where I spoke of the abundant and flamboyant guidance that I am privileged to regularly receive (including cloud-parting spiritual experiences, voices from the Divine, and visits from a man I considered to be a prophet), my mother approached me and commented, "After I hear you talk, I always feel slightly deprived, like why can't these things happen to me?" I was flabbergasted! It was my mother, after all, who had introduced me to sobriety, to Edgar Cayce, and to all the other miracles in my life that have followed in their wake.

I had to mull this over for a day or two, but I soon came to see that Mom *did* have these experiences, just like me. When they happen to her, however, they happen so naturally that she doesn't recognize them as spiritual experiences. She was the first member of our family "guided" into sobriety. Then she was "guided" to bring each of her children into the 12-Step programs. We're miracles in our family—walking, talking miracles. Mom has a legacy of no less than leading ten family members to recovery with over 150 years of cumulative sobriety to date. She introduced me to dream interpretation, all the while accepting her own dream guidance and using it to run her own successful life. How much more divine do experiences need to be? Lightning and burning bushes are no more miraculous than the still, small voice within. It's just that some of us (like Moses and myself) can't *hear* that little voice without more of the fanfare. I'd say that my mother is probably *more* attuned than me, not less—because the universe doesn't have to speak quite so loudly to her as it must with me and as it did with Moses. So in most people the sixth sense is likely to be a quiet knowing, not a bolt of lightning. The lesson here is to trust the process!

The Principles of 12-Step Dreamwork

Many scientists currently believe that the universe consists of twelve elementary particles which are driven by three forces (electromagnetic, strong, and weak). According to them, this is the foundation upon which our physical reality is based. I believe in the operation of serendipity in the universe, so is it any wonder that for program people our spiritual reality is based on twelve elementary *principles* (12 Steps) which are driven by three forces (the spirit, mind/emotions, and body)? Just as scientists pursue knowledge of the physical world to better understand the external universe, we must pursue spiritual knowledge to better understand our internal universe.

What are the principles embodied in the 12 Steps? First, we must know what are the Steps themselves (see fig. 1).

Each one of these Steps can be reduced to one main theme or principle. These will be different for each individual, but for me the 12 Steps reduce to the following:

1. Surrender	7. Humility
2. Hope	8. Courage
3. Faith	9. Restitution
4. Honesty	10. Integration
5. Revelation	11. Guidance
6. Willingness	12. Love and Service

You must find your own understanding of these principles, however, just as you find your own program in the fellowships. I have seen these variants for others:

1. Honesty	1. Powerlessness
2. Hope	2. Acknowledgment
3. Faith	3. Belief
4. Courage	4. Self-Examination
5. Integrity	5. Confession
6. Willingness	6. Surrender
7. Humility	7. Freedom
8. Brotherly Love	8. Courage
9. Discipline	9. Justice
10. Perseverance	10. Consistency
11. Awareness of God	11. Reliance on God
12. Service	12. Usefulness

It is important for you to study each Step and each word in the Step and come to a decision on what main principle it represents for you. Often you may want to meditate and pray first. It is quite helpful to do this with your sponsor or even with like-minded friends from your group. Write down each principle you find and

The 12 Steps[8]

1. We admitted we were powerless over _____ and that our lives had become unmanageable.

2. Came to believe that a Power greater than ourselves could restore us to sanity.

3. Made a decision to turn our will and our lives over to the care of God, *as we understood Him.*

4. Made a searching and fearless moral inventory of ourselves.

5. Admitted to God, to ourselves, and to another human being the exact nature of our wrongs.

6. Were entirely ready to have God remove all these defects of character.

7. Humbly asked Him to remove our shortcomings.

8. Made a list of all persons we had harmed, and became willing to make amends to them all.

9. Made direct amends to such people wherever possible, except when to do so would injure them or others.

10. Continued to take personal inventory and when we were wrong promptly admitted it.

11. Sought through prayer and meditation to improve our conscious contact with God, *as we understood Him*, praying only for knowledge of His will for us and the power to carry that out.

12. Having had a spiritual awakening as the result of these Steps, we tried to carry this message to (others), and to practice these principles in all our affairs.

Figure 1

add them to "Your Dreamwork Glossary" in the back of this book. You may find that as you grow in this program, a Step will come to mean a different principle from what you originally recorded. This is fine and even desirable as this program is a *process*, and new understandings are an indication that you are changing, thus growing.

Once you identify what principles the Steps embody for you, you can begin to correlate the significance of your dreams, visions, and life events with the Step or Steps you are working on. Remember, our program objectives are:

Examine ourselves and be honest (Steps 1, 4, 8, and 10)
Trust and rely on God (Steps 2, 3, 6, and 11)
Take meritorious and moral action (Steps 5, 7, 9, and 10)
Be of service to others (Step 12)

Identifying the principles and correlating them to your Steps is part of processing. It works like this:

1. Process your dream (as described on pp. 49-50).
2. Correlate the principle(s) contained in the dream to the Step to which your dream guidance is referring by asking yourself:
   a. What program objective or objectives are being addressed by the dream?
   b. Is your dream asking you to examine yourself, trust God, take corrective action, or be of service to others?

Answering these questions will help you determine which principle or principles are being addressed by the dream.

The following dream is representative of identifying and correlating the principles in 12-Step dreamwork.

A pipe is in my vagina and my vagina is smoking it. I hoped I wouldn't get addicted to nicotine again.

First, I *recorded* the dream, then I began *processing*. In the processing, I identified that my vagina referred to sex and the smoking referred to addiction. What was the dream *asking* of me? The *answer*, when I considered the four objectives of the program, was that the dream was guiding me to moral action—to NOT do something:

not become addicted to sex. It was asking me to change a defect: desiring an inappropriate sexual liaison. It would require humility for me to admit it and then ask God to remove the presence of this defect. The principle contained in the answer that I *correlated* to my program was humility. By looking at the principles I ascribed to the Steps, I found that I listed humility in the 7th Step. This is clearly a 7th-Step dream for me.

At that particular time in my life, I was consulting with a prestigious institute, and the director and I were wildly attracted to each other. He was married and out of bounds for me, but I felt that if he persisted, I would probably give in. This dream was helping me work on a defect BEFORE I was able to act on it.

Other dreams or series of dreams can get a bit more enigmatic, but with patience we can correlate them to our 12 Steps. Take this example of a dream I had several years ago (clue: I was recording two to six dreams *per night*):

> I received a ticket for five people in the car when there should be four. Then some man gets a ticket for "speeding with reindeer" from *Del Mundo* newspaper.

First, the processing. The ticket is a warning in my dreamwork glossary. Five is the number of change and four is the number of balance (see Part II). A vehicle represents the path I am on. Speeding is obviously "going too fast." Reindeer have always represented Christmas to me, which in my glossary means Christ or Christ Consciousness. *Del Mundo* means "the world" in Spanish and newspaper means news. This is an interpretation of the symbols:

> I am going too fast (speeding) in wanting the changes (number five) brought about by seeking Christ Consciousness (reindeer/Christmas) and am warned (ticket) that the overload of information (news from the whole world) is hard to understand (title in foreign language) and has to be balanced (should be four passengers).

I would like to claim that I transformed this message to significance immediately, but I can't. Its meaning stubbornly eluded me. How can one, especially me, be warned against seeking Christ Consciousness? So I asked for clarification and received this dream the next night:

> I am in school and find a camcorder that records dreams and reviews them. We were looking at all of mine, but the machine jammed with too many dreams. I took out the disks.

I interpreted this dream in this way:

> I am learning (school) by using my dreams and reviewing them. But there are too many (jammed), meaning that I am reviewing too many dreams and "jamming" my comprehension.

When I compared both dreams, I realized that I was out of balance in seeking too much spiritual guidance from my dreams. After all, if we prayed all the time or meditated ten hours a day, we would hardly have time to devote to the rest of our lives. Balance is part of the foundation upon which our lives are built. I asked myself what the objective of my dreams were, and the answer was basically to examine myself—take inventory of my actions. When correlating the principles, I determined that they were 4th-Step dreams. I also saw these as 11th-Step dreams in that they were asking me to rely more on God rather than just on my dreams. They were *guiding* me (my 11th-Step principle) to balance my life.

Making Special Requests

Once we begin working with our dreams, they will guide us and remind us which Steps need to be worked on. Of course, we can take the initiative and request that our dreams help clarify a Step. When we are struggling with working a Step, this can be a very positive and helpful approach. One of the procedures for this is called "Dream Invocation," which is based on the work of Betsy Caprio and Thomas Hedberg. Invoking dreams on particular topics is actually rather easy. Simply put, we just ask for it before falling asleep.

To begin the process of using our dreams as direct guidance to work our 12-Step program of spiritual growth, we can follow the outline (see fig. 2, pp. 52-53) for dream invocation. If at first we don't have much response, we needn't become discouraged. We must simply be persistent and repeat these procedures until our dream life responds to the stated desires of our conscious life. With sincerity and persistence we are sure to see results with a minimum of blockage.

I can illustrate how to use the general procedure outlined above with a dream I had five years ago. I was associated with people who were studying under a great Indian leader, and I was toying with the idea of studying under him, too. Sai Baba is famous for dispensing *vabuti*, an ash-like substance that he reportedly materializes in his hands and gives to people who wait for his appearance at his residence in India. Receiving *vabuti* is supposed to bestow blessings upon the recipient. I decided to invoke a dream about *vabuti*, believing that if *vabuti* were real, I would decide to study Sai Baba. My dream:

> I want *vabuti* to appear and something appears in my palm, but it looks like fool's gold. I suddenly become lucid (aware I'm dreaming) and realize this is my answer, but I don't like it and say, "I want to have a dream about *vabuti*, not fool's gold." Lots of it appears on my palm and I give it away. Someone says that they know Sai Baba has a lot of coal to make this stuff.

This dream was quite clear before I became lucid, but I didn't like the answer. Fool's gold! So the second answer was that I should give it up or give it away. My dream means that, for me, *vabuti* is fool's gold and that Sai Baba makes it from coal. Therefore, I chose not to study under him. However, I believe that, although studying under him isn't appropriate for my spiritual path, it certainly is appropriate for others, as diamonds, too, are made from coal.

Dreams like this one will begin to come naturally as you ask for and invoke them. As you direct your dreams to your 12-Step and spiritual work, they will increasingly speak to you about your pursuits and address clearly your concerns within the realm of your program.

Sequence of 12-Step Dreamwork

To properly use dreamwork in your 12-Step program, you should adapt the following sequence: *Setup, Processing,* and *Acting on the Knowledge.*

- *Setup:* You begin the setup by *expecting* to receive dreams that will be useful to you and *expecting* to remember them. You start by *recording* your dreams, whether in the middle of the night or in the morning. Put a tape recorder or pen/pencil and journal beside your bed and USE them when you awaken. Before drifting to sleep, *talk to your subconscious* and tell yourself what aspect of your program you would like guidance on. Say the *Serenity Dream Prayer* (see fig. 2, p. 53, #3f) at the end of your talk. You may want to use the "Dream Invocation" outline (fig. 2, pp. 52-53), but if not, this setup is as simple as one, two, three:

  1. Expect dreams to be useful
  2. Talk to your subconscious before retiring
  3. Record all dreams or fragments

- *Processing:* Don't begin the dream interpretation and transformation until after your morning has started. Go about your early routine, eat breakfast, do your morning meditation, then sit quietly and begin to decipher the dream.

  The first thing you need to do is to ask yourself which of the four dream categories this dream falls into: *Meaningless, Psychic, Guidance,* or *Reassurance.* Naturally, if it falls into the *Meaningless* or *Reassurance* category, you won't need to go further. If it falls into *Psychic* or *Guidance* categories, you will want to know if your dream can be used in conjunction with your 12-Step work.

  Communication with the dead, memories of past lives, and astral travel dreams probably won't relate to your 12-Step work (but occasionally, even though rare, they may). The next question you must ask yourself is, "Is this dream largely literal?" If the dream shows you eating bowls of cabbage, chances are your higher self is simply instructing you to eat cabbage! Possibly you see yourself going to meetings every night and your dream is simply urging you to do that. These literal dreams are common, so a direct message is the first thing you must look for.

  Once you determine that the dream is not literal and *is* appropriate for 12-Step dreamwork, you must begin to process. After recording your dream in your journal or on your tape recorder, interpret each symbol and symbolic action by using "Your Dreamwork Glossary." Then allow the symbols to resonate within and be transformed into meaningful information. (This is discussed in chapter 2.) Finally, you must correlate your 12-Step principles and find the Step or Steps your dream is addressing. The progression is as follows:

1. Determine the appropriateness of the dream to 12-Step dreamwork
2. Process the dream as described in chapter 2
   a) Interpret the symbols using your glossary
   b) Transform the content into meaningful information
3. Correlate the dream content to principles and Steps (p. 45)

• *Acting on the Knowledge:* Responding to the guidance that you receive is just as important as interpretation and transformation and is actually the last part of processing dreams. I am making a special point of this here because applying what we learn is so vital to successful dreamwork. Remember that "Faith without works is dead." (James 2:17) Is your dream revealing a character defect in you that needs to be changed? Is there someone you need to work with? Do you need to take an inventory? Do you need to study more of your program material? Do you owe someone an apology? Do you need to talk to your sponsor or minister? Do you need to get to a meeting or to join another 12-Step program that you overlooked before? This is a daily program, and you don't want the day to escape before you have done what you can to follow through with the action you were guided to do. The "Big Book" says, "The spiritual life is not a theory. *We have to live it.*"[9]

The vision of spiritual growth for people in recovery that cemented the 12-Step programs into a mainstay of American life is illustrated by their objectives: Examine ourselves and be honest, trust and rely on God, take meritorious and moral action, and be of service to others. This is done on a daily basis and does not leave much room for procrastination and setting aside our spiritual guidance for more "convenient timing."

The purpose of 12-Step dreamwork is to become fully engaged in the development of our potential. We do this by incorporating the Steps of our program with the messages in our dreams and by "practicing these principles in all our affairs." Whether we use a formal invocation to aid the direction of our dreams or simply process the dreams and correlate the principles and Steps with them in a less formal manner is up to us. However we choose to tap into the vast information and guidance from our dreams, visions, and life events, it is a way to rise above the world's unhappiness, unrest, addictions, and criminality. We find serenity, strength, hope, and a constant, never-ending well of power that we need only turn to each and every night of our lives.

Outline for 12-Step Dream Invocation

1. *Choose a Step or topic:* Decide if you want to invoke a dream on a particular Step (usually the one you are working on) or, if you prefer, use a more general approach with an 11th-Step invocation. An 11th-Step invocation is a request for general spiritual guidance through conscious contact, which helps develop the sixth sense, our direct link to God.

Choosing one of the Steps: Usually you will choose to invoke a dream about the Step you are currently working on, whether or not you feel you need dream help with it. If you are having difficulty accepting or understanding a particular Step, then, of course, that is the Step that you would choose to invoke.

Choosing the 11th Step: If you choose to ask for general spiritual guidance in your dreams, rather than help on a particular Step, this would be considered an 11th-Step invocation. This is because the 11th Step is to seek guidance: "Sought through prayer and meditation to improve our conscious contact with God, *as we understood Him*, praying only for knowledge of His will for us and the power to carry that out."

Choosing another topic: Many times you will want to ask for dream guidance about a particular situation, for help in clarifying a principle, to help you pick a sponsor, or to answer a question. You can modify this invocation technique to help you in any area you choose.

2. *Write down the Step or topic* of the dream you are invoking. If this is your first invocation on your chosen topic or with your chosen Step, you must follow these instructions: If you've chosen to work on a Step, write on a blank piece of paper, word for word, the Step you will work on. Under that, write extensively about the Step after discussing it with your sponsor, at meetings, with other program people, or with a therapist, if you have one.

For topics or questions other than Steps: follow the same instructions as above, modifying the procedure as applicable to your topic choice.

If you have worked with this topic or Step before, then you need only write down the topic or Step on a piece of paper and clearly state the point you want clarified. Be sure that you really want to learn the truth. The dream you receive may reveal something you are not comfortable with, but it will present the truth . . . your truth.

3. *Observe these preparations before retiring.*

a) Adapt your bed for sleep, arranging whatever makes you the most comfortable (turning on night lights, fluffing pillows, adding a stuffed animal, or using aromatherapy).

Figure 2

b) Take the paper on which you have written the Step or topic and place it under your pillow.

c) Do some body relaxation techniques: stretching, visualization, or yoga.

d) Read about the Step you have chosen from your main program text ("Big Book," a basic text, *Alanon,* etc.) or from *Twelve Steps and Twelve Traditions.* If you have chosen some topic, read any inspirational literature that applies, including the Bible and other sacred writings.

e) Incorporate the image of the Step or topic into your normal meditation practices.

f) Say the *Serenity Dream Prayer:*

"God, grant me the serenity to accept all guidance revealed through my dreams, the courage to change the things I'm asked to, and the wisdom to interpret according to Your will for me."

4. *Ask to remember all relevant dreams.* As you go to sleep, repeat the Step you are working on and focus on its number. Ask God (as you understand Him), your higher self, or your spiritual guides for help. Ask that you be awakened right after the completion of the dream, no matter what time of the night it is. Then promise yourself that you will write down the dream before returning to sleep! When you do awaken in the night, record the *whole* dream—and don't put it off until morning, or you may forget. Surrender yourself to the process, expect no particular results, and sweet dreams!

5. *Review your dream upon awakening.* When you awaken in the morning, lie still and try to capture any more dreams or fragments of dreams you may have had. Write them down immediately—not after you greet the kids or brush your teeth. Sometimes writing it down will trigger more memory of it. Give thanks for whatever has been given to you and your ability to remember it. Thank any souls who may have aided you in your sleep. Do not interpret your dream at this time.

6. *Process the dream.* Go about your regular morning activities. Prepare for work or school, dress and groom, eat breakfast (if you do), drink coffee (if you do), and complete your morning meditations and readings. Then, bring out your dream, recite your *Serenity Dream Prayer* again, and begin the dream processing. Act on any advice or guidance that you receive. Be sure to discuss your interpretation with your sponsor or at your 12-Step dreamwork group, if you attend one. Remember that using your guidance is VERY IMPORTANT both for continuing to receive helpful dreams and for your spiritual growth.

4

Forming a 12-Step
Dreamwork Group

An article entitled "On Defining Spirit," by Rachael Naomi Remen, was one of the most popular ones ever to appear in the *Noetic Sciences Review.* It was reprinted several times due to reader demand because the information about spirituality was explained so well. In the article, the author differentiates the true nature of spirit and spirituality from mere religiosity. "Religion," Rachael wrote, "is a bridge to the spiritual, but the spiritual lies beyond religion. Unfortunately in seeking the spiritual, we may become attached to the bridge rather than crossing over it."[1] By using dream interpretation with our 12-Step programs, we have the opportunity to cross over this bridge on our path to spirituality, a path that might otherwise become a barrier.

Unfortunately, there are those in our fellowship circles who become attached to the bridge of the program without ever crossing over it into the spiritual. These are the folks that program people call "Big Book Thumpers," the "God Squad," or "Program Nazis." They seem to see things in only black and white. If you don't see things *their* way, then you are wrong. These are the folks who will scoff at your dreamwork—judge your efforts as nonsense or even state that you will never recover if you follow any path but their own. We cannot fault these well-meaning people, but we needn't be confused or disquieted by them either. It is for this reason that we often find it advisable and even necessary to contemplate joining or forming dreamwork groups of our own.

It is no casual suggestion when we challenge you to do dreamwork with others of like mind in an organized group. But how you respond to any of the challenges of 12-Step dreamwork will depend on how you understand your program, your relationship to your recovery, and your relationship to the Divine Forces. It is the crucible of our individual programs that our lives must change by a series of new beliefs, new friends, new insights, and a new depth of relationship to ourselves, our fellow humans, and our Creator.

The most important of these changes will come from the inside out, from the inner realms that affect the changes within and without. It is our individual program and our personal relationship with God that becomes our driving force. But as with any driving force, one needs the fuel to propel it forward. We find that like-minded people in a group situation can become the fuel for our force.

The spiritual principles for healing have been around for eons, but until Bill Wilson found Bob Smith, the doctor who co-founded AA, to work those principles on alcoholism, there wasn't much to fuel the force of recovery. In fact, Bill was close to giving up on the new spiritual approach when he finally met Dr. Bob and formed the first recovery group.

Finding ways to participate with others trudging along our path in life is almost crucial to the success of what we do as humans—groups provide shared meaning, shared solutions, shared commitment, shared challenges, and shared intelligence. From the earliest collection of humans into tribes, to religious congregations, to the Elks, to street gangs, to A.R.E. Search for God study groups, we need each other's love, support, guidance, and understanding. It is called *fellowship* and is a very important aspect of the success in any collective movement or personal change in life style. Look at how many people who have quit drinking on their own . . . only to eventually return to their old life style. Look at how many mothers, fathers, sisters, and spouses who go to a Co-dependents Anonymous (Coda) meeting or two, decide they have the insights needed, quit going, and then catastrophe returns in short measure.

I have a friend, Cherrie. I love her dearly, but like some of us she comes from a fairly messed-up background. So does her husband. Not surprisingly, even though very much in love, they get themselves locked into some rather dysfunctional patterns that often threaten to destroy their happiness. When a crisis hits, he usually attends therapy for a short time and she goes to several Coda meetings. Each will gain some terrific insight, see his or her own faults, get back together, and forget the self-help and support groups altogether—they don't want to be dependent on others. Consequently, they lose the discipline, goal commitment, evolution of common problem solving, and just plain awareness of needed action. They quickly fall into the same crisis patterns and are none the better for it. All this in the name of independence.

Just how we got entrenched as a society in the belief that all dependencies are bad is not readily understandable. We need not be ashamed of our longings to be with and supported by others. I find it highly unflattering when otherwise knowledgeable and supportive persons berate the 12-Step groups as just another dependency. Of course, they are! And proud of it. Is a job a dependency? Is a family structure a dependency? Is church a dependency? Is belonging to a country, county, or city a dependency? Of course. And we are better off as a people for these dependencies. The song, *People*, made popular by Barbra Streisand, states that people who need people are the luckiest in the world. Civilization itself would not have been built if everyone were independent and stood alone. And so to the group process and to dependency on the group process, I pay homage.

Having established the innate value of a group process, let's examine the particular benefits of joining or starting a 12-Step dream group of your own. The first of these benefits, as we mentioned, is *fellowship*. It is just down-right wonderful to associate with like-minded people. We share the same values, goals, and usually talk the same language. We don't feel strange or out of place with "our" people and that is a comfort in itself. Nothing is so uncomfortable as mentioning the need to "surrender" and then have an outsider ask what sport you're into. Equally uncomfortable is mentioning your Higher Power at a community function and having someone begin talking about the movie *Star Wars* and asking if "the Force" is with you. So membership in appropriate fellowships, from the sheer solace of being around your own kind, offers substantial benefits.

Next is *support.* We all need support at times, both emotional and physical. We need people who will assist us in our efforts, encourage us, and allow us to assist and encourage them. Like the stick that breaks easily as one, it can't so easily be broken in a bundle of ten. Our resolve to grow spiritually, practice principles, pray, meditate, and learn from our dreams isn't so easily shoved aside when we have the support and nurturing of a group. We know, from the words of Richard Bach, that we teach best what we most need to learn; and when we can support others by teaching them, we are also teaching ourselves.

There is also the phenomenon of *resistance.* When we delve into our subconscious and attempt to change old destructive patterns, there is a tendency to resist this change. Even if we *want* to work on and improve ourselves, we will be afraid at some level. We are creatures of habit. We are afraid to face defects and fears, afraid of the challenges of an uncertain future, and may desire outcomes different from what is being presented to us in our dreams. The group can give us a kaleidoscope of perspectives that can help us release this resistance. The material and truths that we repress when working by ourselves on dreams can be unearthed in a group setting. The group can provide an "auxiliary consciousness that can see in areas where habitual consciousness is blind. The other people can see things you might overlook," as explained by Robert Bosnak in his book, *A Little Course in Dreams.*[2]

Not all of us, on our own, are willing to expend the energy it takes to gain insights and guidance from our dreams. But in a group setting, the discipline and will to expend this energy are often increased. We come to realize, as we team up, that we can all contribute our own uniqueness, creativity, experience, and strength, and bring honor to each and every dreamer in our sphere. In the team approach we believe that anything is possible and that our programs will benefit tremendously by applying the language of the soul to the principles we are learning in the 12 Steps.

Anatomy of a 12-Step Dreamwork Group

First and foremost, a 12-Step dreamwork group should be run by a group conscience and the 12 traditions of your programs. No one is a leader. Each member is a trusted servant one to the other. The 12 traditions (see the original ones in Appendix IV) as adapted to our dreamwork groups are:

1. Our common welfare should come first; personal progress is better assured with group unity.

2. For our group purpose there is but one ultimate authority—a loving God as He may express Himself in our group conscience. Our leaders are but trusted servants; they do not govern.

3. The only requirement for 12-Step dreamwork group membership is a desire for progress through dreams, visions, and life events processing.

4. Each group should be autonomous except in matters affecting other groups or 12-Step dreamwork groups as a whole.

5. Each group has but one primary purpose: to carry its message to the person who would gain greater understanding through dreams, visions, and life events processing.

6. A 12-Step dreamwork group ought never endorse, finance, or lend our name to any related facility, enterprise, religion, or philosophical/metaphysical position, lest problems of money, property, and prestige divert us from our primary purpose.

7. Every 12-Step dreamwork group ought to be fully self-supporting, declining outside contributions.

8. The 12-Step dreamwork groups should remain forever non-professional, but our service centers may employ special workers.

9. Dreamwork groups, as such, ought never to govern; but we may create service boards or committees directly responsible to those they serve.

10. Our dreamwork groups have no opinion on outside issues; hence our name ought never be drawn into public controversy.

11. Our public relations policy is based on attraction rather than proselytizing; we need to always maintain integrity at the media level.

12. Integrity is the spiritual foundation of all our traditions, ever reminding us to place principles before personalities.

These are simple guidelines that will bond the trustworthiness and purpose of our groups. It is important to understand the meaning and intent of our traditions and hold to them. No group should have a boss; no group should endorse a religion or metaphysical bookstore; no group should forbid membership on the basis of race, creed, philosophy, gender, or religion; no group should meet in someone's house or church without paying rent; no group should make public statements about other types of groups or spiritual practices.

If there is any confusion about the full intent of the 12-Step dreamwork group traditions, it would be wise to read the section of *Twelve Steps and Twelve Traditions* that pertains to Alcoholics Anonymous (see Appendix IV). With little exception, the dreamwork group traditions closely follow and are based on these. And make no mistake, it is recommended that we use these traditions because time and experience have proved that they work.

Also keep in mind that the basis of dreamwork and the basis of assembling together is to enhance our program through love and service to others. It is not for engaging in power trips, enforcing rigid policies, or exercising intolerant attitudes. We must always, as we participate in our dreamwork groups and dream teams, keep principles before personalities and remember that our ultimate goal is service to others. Edgar Cayce said this about groups:

> In all groups, all organizations, it is not what this or that name or group may do, but as *one.* For, the Lord thy God is *one!* And the Christ, the Savior, died for all—*not* for one! no sect, no schism, no ism, no cult.[3]

Getting Started

If you want to begin a 12-Step dreamwork group, place an ad in a recovery or metaphysical newspaper and/or place notices on the bulletin boards of local 12-Step clubhouses. Explain that you're beginning a group on dream interpretation and the 12-Step program and that folks from any 12-Step program interested in dreams are encouraged to join. It shouldn't be long before a number of prospective members have answered.

Ideally, you would want from five to eight people, but if more appear, there are ways to accommodate them with the Dream Team exercises (see "Dream Team Work" on p. 63). These groups should plan on meeting once a week for an hour and a half to enable each member to broaden and deepen his or her 12-Step program on a regular and disciplined basis.

Each person will be expected to carry several supplies to each meeting. Members should always have their personal dreamwork glossary of symbology (see Part II), this book, a 12-Step basic text of their choice (any of the program books such as *Alcoholics Anonymous; Narcotics Anonymous; Emotions Anonymous; Twelve Steps and Twelve Traditions; Young, Sober, & Free; Overeaters Anonymous; Alanon;* etc.), pen and paper, plus any dream or life event they would like to work on. During the meeting, members will be encouraged to jot down insights, to log symbols that strike an inner chord, to make notes of others' dreams that they want to remark on, and to record Dream Team exercises. Members may also want to bring other insightful dream texts and dictionaries. This is a matter for the group conscience, as meetings evolve into unique and creative formats.

12-Step Dreamwork Group Format

As in any successful group endeavor, a prescribed format will work best. First, the chairperson calls the meeting to order. This is followed by a moment of reflective silence, and then the *Serenity Dream Prayer* is recited in unison:

"God, grant me the serenity to accept all guidance revealed through my dreams, the courage to change the things I'm asked to, and the wisdom to interpret according to Your will for me."

Next, have someone read the section "The Purpose of 12-Step Dreamwork" on p. 40 of chapter 3 to the end of the Cayce readings quote on p. 41. This should be followed by reading the group guidelines:

Group Guidelines

1. Each member is asked to honor the integrity and intimacy of this 12-Step dreamwork group by keeping all dreams, revelations, and information strictly confidential among these members. "What you hear in this meeting, let it stay here."

2. Each member is asked to talk about dreams, visions, or life events as they relate to his or her 12-Step program and individual spiritual growth. Each member is asked not to digress to other religious material or metaphysical philosophies unless it directly relates to the group goal of dream interpretation and the 12-Step programs.

3. No one is an "expert" on anyone else's dreams. Each participant is asked not to emphatically declare meanings to others about dream themes, symbology, or how the dream relates to his or her program. Do not say, "This means _____." Speak from your own experience. One might say, "In my glossary this image means _____ ; I learned that the universal meaning for this image is _____ ; I once had a dream in which the symbol of _____ turned out to mean _____ ; according to the Hopi Indians this image means _____ ; when I have a dream about _____ it usually means I need to work on Step _____ ." Although we may be able to shed light on the interpretation of symbols for others, only the dreamers can transform the symbology into meaningful lessons for themselves. We share our experience, strength, and hope. We do not dictate.

4. Use only one dream per meeting, unless the group is either extremely small or two dreams obviously relate to each other in a series. Dreams that run on for pages or involve multiple dreams won't give others a fair opportunity. Be respectful of the time constraints.

The chairperson should now call for a vote on the type of meeting it should be, unless the group uses a previously agreed-upon fixed format. The usual types of meetings are: regular discussion; round robin discussion; half discussion and half dream team; dream team work. The chairperson should then read the corresponding guidelines of the format the group has chosen.

1. *Regular discussion:*   This is when each person is called on or he or she volunteers at random to discuss a personal dream, what he or she believes it means, and/or what the person would like help with. Members are asked not to interrupt, cross talk, or comment while the speaker is talking. When the speaker finishes, another member is either called on by the chairperson or volunteers (if it's a volunteer discussion) and can make a *brief commentary* on the speaker's dream, its symbology, and the Step it might relate to, as long as the person speaks from his or her own experience. Participants are not limited to dreams, but can share visions or life events as well. They can discuss past experiences with dreams, applications of dreamwork, and stumbling blocks to dreamwork. Unless it is a particularly large group, we must try to let everyone share.

2. *Round robin discussion:*   The chairperson calls on the first participant. This participant then discusses a dream, what he or she thinks it means, what he or she understands about its meaning, and what help is desired for understanding it (again, the person doesn't have to discuss a dream, but can share dreamwork concerns in general). Once finished, that person then calls on the next participant. The next member offers his or her insights on the first person's dream or sharing, offers his or her own dream, and finishes by calling on the next person. Each member comments only on the previous dreamer's dream and on no others. If there is time left after the round robin, then open discussion can begin with cross talk allowed.

3. *Half discussion and half dream team:*   This type of meeting is run either like a round robin or discussion for the first thirty-five minutes and the second thirty-five minutes is broken up into dream teams for more individual work. The members regroup for the closing of the meeting.

4. *Dream team work:*   This is when members break up into two- or three-person groups for smaller group work. The chairperson asks for a vote on what type of small group work it will be (options include, but are not limited to, those listed after this format). Then the group breaks up into dream teams and gathers back together for the closing of the meeting.

Ten minutes before closing time, the chairperson calls the meeting to order again. The chairperson then asks, "Does anyone want to share what Step or principle you have correlated this week's dream to and the action you plan to take as a result?" Whoever wants to share does so at this time.

The basket is passed, according to tradition 7, to pay for rent, beverages, snacks, and other group expenses.

The meeting is closed with a meditative silence, prayer, or reflection of the chairperson's choice. (Oftentimes this is the standard *Serenity Prayer* or the Lord's Prayer.)

Dream Team Work

Dream Team Work involves two, sometimes three, people collaborating to do reciprocal dream work. This is particularly helpful because it is often much easier to work with the dreams of others than to work with our own. Just as we can often see others' defects much easier than our own (don't we sometimes overlook the beam in our own eye, while pointing out the motes in the eyes of others?), we can find it easier to jump to the heart of another's dream when he or she is floundering in confusion.

It is for this reason that it is important to take the guidelines for 12-Step dreamwork groups seriously and be sure you understand them. When we learn these exercises, we must always keep in mind, no matter how clear an issue about another seems to us, that the final interpretation always lies with the dreamer, not with the team collaborator. This quote from the Edgar Cayce readings will help to illustrate the importance of this point:

Study—each individual member—to show thyselves approved unto God. *Know,* as has so oft been indicated, oft what may be good for one may be questionable for another. But know that the Lord knoweth His own and calleth them by name.[4]

Listed below are a number of dream team exercises that you will want to practice. Also note that a number of the books listed in the Bibliography contain numerous other dreamwork exercises that you can use. Experiment until you and your members feel comfortable settling on the exercises that work best for the collective soul of your group.

If the group has chosen a Dream Team Work type of meeting and the guidelines have been read and understood, each team will break off and find its own corner of the room. The week's exercise should first be led by one person; in this exercise the other's dream is discussed. Then it should be reversed so that the other leads. Each participant gets a chance to lead on the other's dream and a chance to be led on the processing of his or her own dream. If one of the collaborators does not have a dream, vision, or life event to work on during this turn, he or she should work the following exercises to personally increase the dream glossary, pinpoint the 12-Step principles, and/or dialogue with a "wise dream interpreter," as described below.

Dream Team Exercises:

Role Playing: In chapter 2 we discussed dialoguing by imagining a conversation with a dream figure, a wise dream interpreter, a spiritual guide, or any dream symbol. Role playing is another creative method for "dialoguing" with a dream symbol to discover the meaning or purpose of its involvement in your dream. Each member shares his or her dream with the other and takes notes on the other's narration in order to ask pertinent questions during the interchange portion of your Dream Team Work. One member of the team picks a dream figure or symbol that seems important from the dream that has just been shared. Maybe it is a pine tree, a space ship, an elderly woman, or a pool of water.

If you pick the pine tree, for example, imagine your roots in the ground, smell the sweet odor of the forest, feel the wind rippling through your needles—pretend you are the symbol and, of course, pretend you can speak. Become that image. Imagine yourself to be like one of those visual effects in science fiction movies—you can take any shape or form you want. Your collaborator now begins a dialogue with this symbolic figure and records the answers on *your* pad of paper. He or she will ask questions like: Why did you appear in_____'s dream? What does your color signify? Why did you say _____ in this dream? What insight are you bringing to this person? What Step are you asking him or her to pay attention to? And so on. Very often the spontaneous answers you give will prompt more questions and dialogue from your collaborator. Your dream team partner can help uncover inner aspects and ask questions that you would not have thought of, giving you a whole new slant on your dream message.

Another form of role playing is for one member to play the role of a "wise dream interpreter." We discussed in chapter 2 how one can do this exercise alone by imagining the dialogue. But in this exercise, a person plays the role of the "wise dream interpreter," while the collaborator asks questions and records the answers in the role-player's notebook.

This exercise can be used to interpret a particular dream or it can be used for dream and program information in general. The collaborator will ask appropriate questions and the person playing the role will answer and instruct. The important point to remember for the "wise dream interpreter" is not to censor the answers. Let them flow spontaneously, even if silly, because these could lead to valuable information on one's personal symbology. The collaborator will always record the questions and answers in *your* notebook for further study later.

At the end of each dialogue, the collaborator will thank the image or figure for talking to them. "Thank you, tree symbol, for helping us here today." This reinforces and encourages active participation from the person's subconscious for future sessions.

Guided Imagery (through dream reentry): In guided imagery one member of the dream team will lie supine on a mat or on the floor, close the eyes, take some deep breaths, and slowly reenter the dream of his or her choice. This is done by remembering the original dream setting and starting the dream over mentally. The one attempting to reenter a dream should try to reignite the visual and sensory reality as best he or she can. Even if the imaginatory dream impressions are vague, the person should continue because as the collaborator asks questions and probes further, the answers will seemingly pop into the "dreamer's" mind.

As "the dreamer" reenters, he or she shares out loud the reality and the events of the dream. The collaborator must imagine the inner space of the dream along with the partner. Once the dream sharing is finished, the collaborator begins asking questions of the "dreamer," who remains supine with eyes closed. The "dreamer" may be asked to notice the color of the clothes, building, or vehicle. The collaborator can ask the partner what sounds he or she hears, what odors are present, or how the dreamer feels about a particular occurrence.

The "dreamer" may be instructed to ask a question of a dream figure; for example, a dog: "Ask that little dog what he is doing there."

If the person is fleeing someone, the collaborator may ask the "dreamer" to confront that figure: "Why are you chasing me?" The "dreamer" may be instructed to find a solution by extending the dream: "How can you get this person to stop chasing you?" Again the collaborator must record all the answers being given in the dreamer's own notebook. Once the collaborator feels that all the illuminating information has been given, he or she will inquire, "What is this dream asking of you?" Finally, the collaborator asks, "What objectives from the program does this dream ask of you: to examine yourself and be honest, trust and rely on God, take meritorious and moral action, or be of service to others?"

Once the questions are answered, the dreamer can sit up and the team discusses what principle and Step or Steps might be involved.

Sentence Completion: This exercise can be geared toward the interpretation of one particular dream or can be used to work with symbology in general. One collaborator of the team shares a dream or describes several symbolic images or actions that he or she wants help in deciphering. The other person then writes three to five sentences in the first person's notebook. For instance, if the dreamer had a funny dream about a blue banana in a bowl of cherries, the collaborator may write: "Another word for banana is _____ "; A bowl of cherries reminds me of _____ "; "The color blue makes me feel _____ "; "A saying about a banana is_____." " The dreamer then takes back his or her notebook and fills in the blanks.

The dreamer might answer that "Another word for banana is 'fruit' "; "A bowl of cherries reminds me of 'life isn't a bowl of cherries' "; "The color blue makes me feel 'sad' "; "A saying about a banana is 'he's going bananas.'" It wouldn't be too difficult to interpret this, for example, as a person who is afraid that depression is the basis of his or her fear of going insane. Such a dream would probably be asking the dreamer to trust God. It would, therefore, be considered a 2nd-Step dream. This simple "funny" dream suddenly illuminates a whole series of symbology for this dreamer.

But again, the collaborator mustn't tell the dreamer what the dream is saying. The dreamer must do his or her own processing. Correct answers will always be in an individual context. For instance, what if this same dream came from a teen-age girl? Her answers to the statements might be, "Another word for banana is 'penis' . . . 'pop your cherry' . . . 'blue is the color of honesty' . . . A saying about a banana is 'the ditty from the Chiquita® banana advertisements.' " This young woman might be getting an important message about her virginity. Maybe she is playing "sexy," like the Chiquita banana girl, while not telling the young man she is dating that she is a virgin. In this case, the dream is asking her to be honest and examine her own behavior; it might be an 8th- and 9th-Step dream. It is very important for us to remember who the processor is as we do these exercises. It is the *dreamer,* not the collaborator.

Word Association: One exercise for word association is the "machine gun questions" technique. This is a fun drill in which the questioner listens to the dream of the first party, then in rapid succession asks what each symbol means. "What does _____ mean?" The dreamer answers quickly, without thinking about it first. Next the questioner quickly asks what the first answer means, then what the next answer means. They do this about three times for each symbol that needs clarification. An example of this comes from Lisa, a young woman who was having a difficult time understanding why in a certain dream she was afraid of pregnancy. I shot the question at her, "What does *pregnancy* mean to you? NOW! Answer!"

"Child," Lisa said.

"What does *child* mean to you? NOW!"

"Life," she said.

"What does *life* mean to you?"

"Sober life," and she smiled and added, "It's a gift."

From this we determined that Lisa was afraid of this new sober life, this gift from God. She was frightened, like many of us, about the uncertainty of a new life that was so different from the old. From that "machine gun question" session, the full meaning of her dream revealed itself. The point of this technique is to rapidly fire the questions at your partner and not allow him or her time to think about or censor the answers. It allows the subconscious to answer.

Past, Present, and Future Technique: In this exercise, one team member will present a dream to the collaborator. The collaborator then will interpret the dream from his or her own perspective (not saying this IS what it means, only what it means *to the collaborator*). The dream is interpreted three times, *each from a different perspective.* The first interpretation is done as if the dream contains a message from the dreamer's past, the second as if it contains a message about the present, and third as if it contains a message about the future. The dreamer takes notes from the interpreter who can help clarify precognitive or other angles of the dream that the dreamer may not have considered.

Stumbling Blocks for Group Members to Observe

Each member working with a dreamwork group should endeavor to avoid a number of stumbling blocks that can impede success either personally or for others in the group. Foremost, group members must try not to become attached to preexistent conceptions about what symbols mean. It is fine to use dream dictionaries as starting points for interpretation, but don't take them as gospel. We all must have our own glossary of terms in addition to the universal and cultural meanings that we find in dream dictionaries. As we described in chapter 2, a symbol's universal or cultural meaning may be how we interpret it, or we may have a very personal and different understanding. Sometimes, symbols change their meaning from dream to dream.

A striking example of this comes from my own dreams about snakes, a symbol that for me frequently alternates meanings. The universal meaning of the snake is akin to cold-blooded, crawling-on-the-belly creatures or sexual connotations, such as a phallic symbol. Metaphysical or spiritual symbology is often borrowed from the Indian religions where a snake can represent wisdom. The Judeo-Christian-Islamic influences suggest that snakes represent temptation and evil.

I have had dreams on many occasions in which the symbols could be understood from all these sources. Long ago I had a dream that fat, red-and-black-striped snakes were under my bed. I couldn't get to the door and had to crawl out my window. These snakes were warning me (red) about my darker nature (black) and sexual issues (snakes under the bed) that I was having a hard time escaping from.

Another dream presented me with an image of a huge black snake that crawled under my breast as I lay on a path. This particular snake represented evil and was telling me that evil touched my heart (under my breast) because I had neglected my mission in life (lying down on my path), but the evil was not long with me (snake leaving). Years later I had another dream in which I was crossing a desert and found a snake on a little knoll. It was gold colored and had diamond eyes and sang for me. This snake represented the wisdom I would be learning in what I thought was a dry (desert) time in my life. Not too long ago, I dreamt:

> There were two green cartoon snakes talking to each other about how silly humans are. "You just rattle a little bit and they go into a panic," one snake laughed. The snakes then turned into *real* snakes and laid their heads on my breast. I was very careful not to move, lest they bite and kill me.

These snakes represented two corporate men I worked with who often scoffed at the "little" people they were expected to help. I had taken steps to draw attention to their superiors about their shabby treatment of others, but because of their youth, I had a tendency not to take them seriously. The dream was warning me that they weren't harmless cartoon characters, although they acted like them, but men who could be dangerous to me. The green signified that they and I would grow from the situation, but I was not to make another move against them lest I be bitten. It is interesting to note that they were on my bare breast, and both men had made sexual passes at me!

So, even though you have an entry in your glossary for a certain symbol, you must continue to explore new meanings for that symbol and always remember to record them in "Your Dreamwork Glossary."

We are all experts on dream interpretation—our own! There will be times, though, when we are tempted to do the dreamwork of others and this, too, is a stumbling block to be avoided in dreamwork groups. Often, we come up with a valid meaning and the other person agrees. Then it happens again, and soon that person is coming to you regularly for dream interpretation. If that individual is not willing to do the work, you mustn't be doing it for that person. Becoming an expert for others can be a stumbling block for them because it can stunt their growth. Additionally, it can be a stumbling block for you because it can create an ego-inflation problem that impedes your growth! Helping others is wonderful—to get over a slump, decipher one dream, get to the meaning of a troublesome symbol—but to take over for them and become their expert is not wise for either of you.

Although we have sponsors in our regular 12-Step programs who *are* the experts for us, the sponsors in dreamwork do not assume the same authoritative place. A sponsor in AA or other groups is someone who has been around longer than their "baby," and the "baby" begins working the program of the sponsor until he or she develops a program of his or her own. In dreamwork groups, the sponsor doesn't have to be an "old-timer" nor a dream-processing expert. A sponsor in a dream group simply becomes a more permanent dream team member. Usually members sponsor each other. You might call a dream sponsor regularly and he or she can do the word association or sentence completion with you, quickly over the phone, to aid in your dreamwork. It's a reciprocal relationship, enjoyable, useful, but never dictatorial nor assuming the position of "expert."

A common pitfall when failing to understand the significance of our dreams is the influence of wish fulfillment. We want a particular outcome to an issue and so "read" the desired outcome into our dream images. In 1991, while in the Yukon, I met a man with whom I became romantically smitten. I wanted to be in love with him and have him fall in love with me. So when I had a dream about going on a road and finding it barricaded, the obvious interpretation was, "This relationship is not the right path." But since I didn't want to see that, I transformed it to, "My old path was barricaded to make way for the new one with David."

My subconscious does not give up easily, so I had another dream in which the road I was on was barricaded because it was being reconstructed. The correct "read" was, "A different way is being prepared for you." My wish-fulfillment transformation, however, became, "My guides are building a new path for my new relationship with David." Finally I had this dream:

I was in a hot tub, naked. A bunch of businessmen came in. A male friend sat in front of me to "cover" me while a second went to get my suit. It was plain black. I put it on under the water, then stepped out. I noticed that I had the suit on inside out, laughed, and told him I had to change it, which I did.

This dream was telling me that I was in hot water and vulnerable (naked). The rational side of me (businessmen) was closing in. Part of me was trying to protect (cover) my vulnerability. I was hiding the truth (putting on a *black* suit) from myself because I was under the influence of my emotions (putting the suit on under water). I was also "twisting" or getting the information backward (putting the suit on backward). I realized I'd have to change my attitude and laughed at my stubbornness. Finally the message came through. This dream was asking me to honestly examine myself. It was a 10th-Step dream.

In our dreamwork groups, we also sometimes have trouble with sense prejudices. In other words, the collaborator or dreamer may constantly refer to only one of the senses in asking questions or drawing attention to images. For example, he or she may keep asking what you "think" of this color or phrase or dream figure, when what is also needed to be asked is, "What do you hear?" "How does it taste?" "Can you feel the fabric?" "What is the color of that house?" Remember, we can also ask, "What does the house sound like?" or "Can you describe how the feeling looked?"

Mixing the senses can often aid us in breaking patterns in our interrogations on dream material. Possibly you had perceived no color or sound in a dream. But in a dream-reentry exercise, you could "imagine" what might have been there and notice things you didn't notice the first time around. So, if you rely too heavily on any one of the senses like sight, ask your collaborator to switch to questions about sound, feel, taste, and thoughts. If you get entrenched in one style or form of questioning, try to mix the senses to get a fresh perspective.

We can also overlook the helpfulness of searching for multiple meanings in our dreams. Although no one knows exactly why we dream in parables, metaphors, and analogies, one of the suggested explanations is that a dream can be speaking to us on more than one level. That singular dream can be telling us something about our health and at the same time talking about a defect of character that needs altering.

Imagine a man has a dream in which a female co-worker of his offers him a piece of lemon pie. He takes the pie from the woman and it tastes like rat poison. Then she says, "Remember, I have the Sioux Indians to take care of me." The dream could be telling this man that he is overweight and his eating is out of place (eating in the office), and his wild (Indian) appetite is poisoning his system (rat poison). Another simultaneous meaning could be a warning to him about this co-worker, who happens to be named Sue, who flirts with him (offers sweets, pie), an action which is a real lemon to him. She will turn into a rat and eventually sue (Sioux) the company in a particularly savage manner. The dream would be warning him not to respond to her attentions because of her future malevolent intentions. Dreams can, and often do, operate on several levels. The person who is new to dream interpretation shouldn't be concerned with multiple levels of meaning from the start, but the seasoned dream processor needs to stay open to the possibilities.

The main task of our 12-Step program is to become whole, functional, and integrated human beings. We respond to life based on our internal qualities, whether we are conscious of those qualities or not. The 12-Step programs have a way of pulling our qualities into the light and showing us if they are worthy of our spiritual life or if they need to be brought into attunement with a higher value.

In a similar manner, our dreams have a way of pulling our qualities into the light and showing us if they are worthy, too. Doing this work in a dreamwork group setting will help each program member to better identify the qualities he or she wants and needs to be examining in a supportive and loving atmosphere. In addition, dreamwork, when done with others of a like mind, will enhance both the working of our Steps and understanding of our dreams, as well as accelerate our spiritual growth.

In Part III, we will begin to familiarize ourselves with the universal and cultural meanings of many symbols so that we can discover our personal understandings of dream images. We will begin the practice of recording symbols in order to build our own personal glossary, which will be the most important dream dictionary we will ever possess.

In Part III, we will read and study the dreams of many program people from around the world. We will learn, by example, just how processing dreams and correlating them to the 12 Steps works.

As we move forward along our chosen spiritual path, we remember always that the three free tools for attunement with the Higher Source are prayer, meditation, and dreams. In prayer we talk to God; in meditation we listen; in dreams we communicate.

PART II

YOUR DREAMWORK
GLOSSARY AND HOW TO USE IT

Your Dreamwork Glossary

Many of the images, night specters, puns, and behaviors exhibited in your dreams will never be found in a dream dictionary, however comprehensive, because they are uniquely formed by *your* subconscious mind. In this dreamwork glossary, a dream dictionary that you create for yourself, you will begin to record and define the symbols and symbolic behaviors that present themselves in your dreams, visions, and life events. It takes discipline and devotion to become familiar with the symbolic language that your subconscious uses, and this glossary is designed to help you do that.

In chapter 2 there is a comprehensive overview of this glossary (pp. 25-33). You may want to review that section now, before proceeding.

"Your Dreamwork Glossary" contains twelve symbol categories under which you will eventually record your dream images. Each category section begins with a description of the positive and negative meanings of the symbols and the behaviors related to that category. The brief introductory description will help you understand how the category images connect with the universal definitions ordinarily found in other dream dictionaries and listed in this glossary as well.

Following the introductory description is a list of related idioms and sayings that Western, English-speaking society commonly uses. These aphorisms depict the many ways in which we view various objects and behaviors. Familiarizing yourself with them can demonstrate ways in which your subconscious mind may choose to talk to you.

Next you will find a list of words, with definitions, that fit into that grouping. The interpretations of the symbols listed here are gathered from the Edgar Cayce readings, Carl Jung's understanding of the collective unconscious, Linda Goodman's description of the Chaldean-Hebrew-cabalistic understanding of numbers, and the 12-Step program principles. I have tried to keep the definitions as "universally" objective as possible. However, some of the definitions given may contain unintended "Western" connotations. In any case, I have called the section "Universal Meanings."

These universal meanings will give you a sense of what the symbols in that grouping typically refer to. From them you may formulate other definitions of words that belong in, but are not listed in, this section. These universal definitions are not necessarily what you will write down as you build your glossary of dream terms, although they may be.

After the "Universal Meanings" you will find your personal glossary format. Here, in the blank lines provided, you will record your dream images—either symbols or symbolic actions. Notice that the blank line beside where you record your image is divided into two sections: Cultural Meaning and Personal Significance.

You are to supply what you believe to be the cultural meaning of the words as well as your own specific, unique understanding. The "cultural" meaning can come from many sources. Generally this source will depend upon the major influences in your self-identity. This may include your education, background, sexual orientation, living environment, race, religion, etc. Frequently, the "cultural" meanings we associate with images will vary, depending on the dream context, our age, and our current environment. Sometimes we will see the influence of Western culture in an image, the pop culture, Indian culture, Southern culture, gay culture, or some other significant influence. You must be flexible when deciphering the "cultural" meanings, remembering that this is multivariant and dependent upon current circumstances and mind-sets.

Your personal definitions are individual impressions that are totally dependent on how you view the world, not how a whole class of people views the world. For instance, your preferences for color will determine your personal understandings of them. Blue *universally* means infinity and truth, in the Judeo-Christian *culture* it usually means Christ, and in Russian street *culture* it means homosexual. If you have no particular reaction to the color, then the universal or cultural definitions may be enough for you. However, if you *hate* the color blue, then your Personal Significance will be listed as "distasteful, ugly, or hated."

You will use these categories only after you have recorded your dream and want to start the processing. For each image or behavior that you want to record, you will look up the category that it most likely falls into. Review the introductory text, idioms, and universal meanings, then list your image and the definitions, as you understand them.

The first three categories—elements, colors, and numbers—are the most important in terms of understanding your dream symbols. This is because they clarify the purpose, quality, and virtue of the symbols found in the other categories. For instance, a shoe might represent a foundation for you—but what kind? The color of the shoe—blue—can help give the image definition. A blue shoe may mean that a foundation of honesty or Christ Consciousness is needed in your personality. A size-*twelve* blue shoe, then, could mean that this Christ-like foundation should be built upon the 12 Steps or the 12th Step itself.

The symbols you will study and list in the remaining categories are the infrastructure for the message content or lessons contained in the dream, vision, or life event. They will impart the full meaning and intent of the messages as you process your dreams. While these last nine categories actually are the dream, the first three categories primarily describe the qualities of the images found in the dream.

As you begin to build your glossary, be creative and flexible. For even as the "cultural" source on which you rely for your definitions will alternate, so, too, will your personal understandings change. In addition, as you search for the meanings of evolving dream images, don't forget to use the exercises in chapters 2 and 4 to uncover meanings. As you use and build "Your Dreamwork Glossary," it will quickly become more useful to you than any other dream dictionary in existence.

You stand at the crossroads of imagination and self-understanding in creating this glossary. It is the interpretations contained herein that will allow your imagination to become the self-understanding upon which you will build a recovered self, a spiritual self, and a greater self. And, by the grace of God, as you practice processing your dreams, with the help of this glossary, your dreams will become a source of spiritual awakening, even as you sleep!

The Four Elements: Earth, Water, Air, and Fire

According to the ancient Greek philosophers, the four elements of earth, air, fire, and water were the primal substances which formed the world. Although we now know that microscopic particles and charges, such as photons, neutrinos, and quarks, are among the smallest particles that compose our universe, they just don't lend themselves to the same rich analogies that come to us from the Grecian age. The four elements bring us such opulent expressions as "Mother Earth," "the sea of life," and the "whirlwind romance," while "Mother Photon," "the neutrino of life," and "whirlquark romances" are sayings whose time has not yet arrived in our society. So, although we know that the four elements are not the elementary particles of our universe, for purposes of the language from our superconscious we will allow the simplicity.

The four simple elements embody most of nature and naturally overlap in various interpretative settings. For instance, a rain storm is both air and water. As you decide which part of the glossary to use, you must establish what the emphasis of your image was. If it was the blowing turbulence of the storm, then "air" would be the category of choice. However, if the downpour seemed the most prevalent aspect of the image, then you would pick the "water" category. Even the act of deciding which category to use for a given symbol or symbolic action can be the first steps to interpretation.

Earth

Positive Meanings: The earth represents the practical, stable, "down to earth," and feet-on-the-firm-ground type of model. For many, earth signifies a firm foundation or the need for a firm foundation. Mountains can represent strength or spiritual heights. The earth reflects our physical self or body, our carnal natures, our life on earth, and materialism. We plant things in Mother Earth for future nourishing, and we build houses from her bounty for our protection and comfort. She is feminine, supportive, our comfort, our mother.

Negative Meanings: Dirt may reveal debasement of character or "dirty thoughts." A muddy road can indicate that one is on the wrong path. Being alone on a mountain can represent separation or isolation from our fellow humans. A ditch can warn you to "ditch" something or mean you are getting stuck in a rut. Climbing a mountain can mean the need to overcome carnal obsessions. Earthquakes denote the shaking of our foundation, any earthshaking event. Volcanoes often represent repressed emotions. Holes and caves can denote hidden information from the bowels of the earth. If images plunge into the earth, they can mean our subconscious or our past.

Related Idioms: "They have a dirty mind," "Earthborn," "Earthbound," "Dust heap," "Dirt poor," "Clear as mud," "Dry as a desert," "Don't make a mountain out of a molehill," "Don't burrow in a hole," "Don't blow your top," "Here's mud in your eye," "The good earth," and "The meek shall inherit the earth."

Universal Meanings: Boulders (barriers), caves (subconscious or past), clay (creativity in raw form), cliffs (make a decision), comet (tremendous creative potential), deserts (need for substance), dirt (dirty thoughts or actions), dust (unclear thoughts or neglect of something), earth (grounded or firm foundation), earthquakes (warning of immanent shake-up in life), minerals (spiritual strengths), mountains (spiritual aspirations), mud (see "dirt"), quicksand (losing all); rocks (solid foundations or casting stones), sand (time or elusiveness), steppes (usually refers to medieval times), valleys (dips in life events), and volcanoes (repressed or volatile emotions).

EARTH

Symbol	Cultural Meaning	Personal Significance

Water

Positive Meanings: All life sprang from the ocean and thus the ocean often symbolizes our Creator. "Mother Earth" could just as easily be coined "Mother Ocean." A river often refers to Christ, as in His baptism, while the river currents can refer to God's will. Water is ruled by the color blue and means truth. Dreams of swimming can imply spiritual progress. To drink is to drink from the river of life or quench a great thirst. Water is of the spirit, but for many dreamers refers to emotion as well. Crossing a river or the sea in a boat can refer to crossing over to the other side, as in physical death.

Negative Meanings: Drowning can mean that one is in spiritual trouble. Falling in a river is usually a warning of some sort, either of a spiritual crisis or emotional problem. Snow is frozen water and can mean frozen emotions or a warning about spiritual inactivity. A boiling pot or hot water means to change the activity it is associated with. Dams refer to the holding back of emotions. Flood waters, tidal waves, typhoons are warnings about events, either personal or global.

Related Idioms: "All washed up," "Getting into hot water," "Ice water in their veins," "Snow job," "Up the river," "Laughing water," "Misty-eyed," "You're in deep water," "Wishy-washy," "White as the driven snow," "Drink up a river," "Dammed up," "Sail down the river," "Dull as ditch water," "I feel swimmingly," and "Don't rain on my parade."

Universal Meanings: Bathtubs (clean up), canals (birth canal or narrow direction), creeks (beginning spirituality or feeding emotions), dams (controlling emotions), floods (uncontrolled emotions), fountains (of youth), hail (see "snow"), ice (frozen emotion, isolation), iceberg (only the tip of the problem is known), lakes (serenity), mist (unclear), oceans (source of life), pools (emotion), puddles (annoyances), rain (replenishing), rivers (life), seas (see "oceans"), snow (emotionally cold or untouched), springs (see "wells"), storms (anger and temper), tears (warning of impending grief), washing machines (clean up your image), waterfalls (expression of emotions), waves and tidal waves (being hit with emotions), and wells (inner reserves, deep ideals).

WATER

Symbol	Cultural Meaning	Personal Significance

Air

Positive Meanings: Air usually represents mental activity or spiritual ideals. "Light as air" can refer to the imagination. Air is also the "breath of life," and breathing air into something can mean integration into a higher consciousness. Flying can mean wishful thinking, astral travel, attaining high ideals, or a note to rise above the problem. Air dreams also include such elusive things as rainbows, microwaves, TV, and radiowaves.

Negative Meanings: Tornadoes or turbulent air often denote mental breakdowns or overwrought minds. One can be "blown away" by the wind or be warned about a fight ahead by dreaming of a storm. "Hot air" warns of puffing one's self up with false claims. Clouds, which are at the whim of air currents, denote a person easily swayed. Dreams of space could be denoting a "spacey" person.

Related Idioms: "The sky's the limit," "Full of hot air," "Light as air," "Breezy personality," "Bluster," "A lofty air," "Windbag," "Up to the stratosphere," "Castles in the air," "Firmly planted in the air," "Into thin air," "Gone with the wind," "Vent your feelings," "Like sand against the wind," "Stinks to high heaven," "Head in the clouds," and "The winds of change."

Universal Meanings: Airbags (protection), balloons (unrestricted), breath (breath of life), breeze (easy does it), clouds (easily swayed, illusory, or vague), cosmos (greatly expanded spiritual awareness), eye of the hurricane (as much trouble is to come as has been), hot air (posturing), hurricane (sudden change; see "storms"), microwaves (inner passions), music (harmony or discord), odors (quality of an experience, does it stink or is it pleasant?), ozone (protection), rainbows (perfect harmony or God's promise to us), rain clouds (depression or emotional downpour coming), space (inability to concentrate; see "cosmos"), storms (temper or warning of quarrel to come), stratosphere (highest earth consciousness), thunder (an announcement to get your attention), tornadoes (see "hurricane"), TV and radio signals (message to come), whirlwinds (confusion), windmill (working with the will of God), and vacuums (void inside).

AIR

Symbol	Cultural Meaning	Personal Significance

Fire

Positive Meanings: Fire can denote passion, as in one is "on fire" with the program. Fire signifies a process of transformation, the end of the old and beginning of the new—as the phoenix rising from the ashes. It can forewarn of messages from God like with Moses and the burning bush and St. Paul blinded by the light on the road to Damascus. Fire is a preparation—to cook something is to prepare it. Fire keeps us warm and keeps the wild animals at bay.

Negative Meanings: Fire burns! It can mean an immediate need for purification. People burned anything associated with the plague to purify it. It can warn against indulging in "fiery emotions," like jealousy, vengeance, hatred, and unbridled sensuality. We can burn with anger or be hot tempered, and we don't want to "burn" others with our character defects.

Related Idioms: "Don't play with fire and you won't get burned," "Fuel the fires," "Brief as lightning," "S/he's not too bright," "Tongue of fire," "Better to marry than to burn," "Got the hots for you," "The coals of revenge," "To carry a torch for someone," and "To wish upon a star."

Universal Meanings: Ashes (humility or something to rise from), bombs (you are going to be surprised by something), burning bushes (message from the Divine), campfires (quick cleansing of attitude needed), cauldrons (seething emotions), coals (a hidden emotion exists), daylight (consciences), electricity (life force and/or God's will), embers (a spark is still alive), explosions (loss of control), fire (need for purification), fireflies (childlike wonder), fireplaces (warmth and security), flame (warning not to get burned), forest fires (warning, raging emotions; see "fire"), guns (sexual problems or sabotage), hell (fear of damnation), holocaust (purified), lava (suppressed emotions erupting), light (spiritual light; see "daylight"), light bulbs (clarity of thoughts or situation), lightning (flashes of insight, revelation), matches (power to destroy), moonlight (unconscious contact, hope, or romance), pyromaniac (an all-consuming character defect), smoking (warning of danger), stars (enlightenment or celebrity), stoves (prepare yourself), sun (Christ—as in Son of God), sunlight (conscious contact), sunrise (dawn of consciousness), and sunset (close to the end).

FIRE

Symbol	Cultural Meaning	Personal Significance

Colors

Experts used to claim that dogs could see only in black and white, but eventually learned years later what dog lovers always knew—man's best friend *does* see in color. Experts have also surmised many things about dreaming in color or black and white, such as: men are more likely to dream in black and white, women in color; and dreaming in color is relatively rare. Today we understand that these experts didn't understand the underlying mechanisms of dreaming. Color is used in dreamtime to heighten one's awareness about the meaning of symbols or symbolic actions. It is not a question of dreaming in color or not, it is a question of whether one *notices* the color of something in a dream, vision, or life event.

When the dreamer's subconscious is attuned to the vibrations of color, then it will use color in the communication of symbology. If the dreamer is not attuned to color significance, then color will not be noticed or emphasized. If your dreams haven't been using color as a normal part of their symbolic language and you would like to add this dimension to your dream symbol vocabulary, there are two methods for doing this.

1. Read over this section on color several times so that your subconscious becomes used to the universal meanings of the colors. Soon your higher self will draw on this source of knowledge.

2. During your dreamwork as a member of a dream team, for example, when you reenter a dream, have your team partner ask what the color of various objects are. Immediately your imagination (guided by your higher self) will ascribe colors to the objects asked about. You will shortly begin to notice colors *during* your dreams, because your subconscious will then know it is important to you. Your mind, or more precisely your *superconscious* mind, wants to please you. Once it knows you want something, it will do all in its power to accommodate your wishes.

The clearer the color, the clearer its reference for interpretation. Muddy or dark colors usually refer to ill health or negative emotions. Daylight and brightness can denote clarity of intent and thought and also be associated with spiritual uplifting and God, *as we understand Him*. Darkness and night can be something that is not yet known to a person, something emerging from the subconscious, or something someone is hiding from you, or the inability to see clearly. Pastels ordinarily refer to the feminine aspect of the self, innocence, or babyish attitudes and behaviors.

After reading the general, more universal (sometimes cultural) meanings of each of the colors below, examine your own likes, dislikes, and past associations. As the colors come up in your dreams, assign deeper, clearer, more personal meanings for future reference.

Related Idioms: "That's a horse of a different color," "Color blind," "Off-color," "Stick to your colors," "Passed with flying colors," "The experience colored their views," "Color on the cheeks," and "Flying your colors."

Universal Meanings:

Black: mystery, secrets, or hiding; darkness of thought; death; evil or sin; mourning; depression or gloom; character defects.

Related Idioms: "Black-tie events," "Black-balled," "Blackouts," "Black as the ace of spades," "Black holes," "Black is beautiful," and "Black hearts."

Black and White: right and wrong; good and evil; positive and negative; impurity.

Related Idioms: "Salt and pepper," "It's not a black and white issue," "It's in black and white," and "Black men are pearls in beauteous women's eyes."

Blue: Christ Consciousness; truth; peace; fidelity; infinity.

Dark Blue: deceit and lies; secrets; depression and gloom.

Related Idioms: "Blue laws," "Blue chips," "Blueprints," "Blue collar," "Talking up a blue streak," and "He/she has the blues."

Brown: earthy, practical, and stable; grounded; materialistic nature; attachment to the earth plane.

Dark Brown: depression; regression; muddy and unclear; shitty situation; lasciviousness or perversions.

Related Idioms: "Brown outs," "To do it up brown," "Brown nosing," and "Brownie points."

Gray: brain or intellect; maturity; wisdom: strength.

Dark Gray: ill health; depression; boredom; fear.

Related Idioms: "Gray markets," "Gray days," and "Gray issues."

Green: growth and vitality; healing; inexperience; envy; jealousy.

Dark Green: sickness of the body.

Related Idioms: "Green power," "Green rooms," "Green Peace," "He's still green," "Green-eyed monster," and "Green thumb."

Orange: health; energy; vibrancy.

Rust: possible heart disease; stagnation.

Related Idioms: "Agent orange," "Peaches and cream," and "He's got rust in his pipes."

Pink: love, joy, and happiness; good health; optimistic attitude.

Hot or Neon Pink: passion; hot sex.

Pale Pink: weakness; immaturity; childish things.

Related Idioms: "Pink-eyed," "Pinkos," "In the pink," "Looking through rose-colored glasses," and "Pink elephants."

Purple: royalty; power; the highest spiritual color.

Violet: healing power.

Related Idioms: "Purple heart," "Purple people eater," and "Sweet violet."

Red: life force and new life; warning; need for purification; anger and aggression; temper.

Maroon: abandoned or stranded; drab; poor health; negative attitude.

Related Idioms: "Red coats," "Seeing red," "Red faced," "Red Cross," "Not a red cent," "Marooned," and "Paint the town red."

White: purity; "clean," as in "off drugs"; innocence; wisdom; virginal; illumination.

Off-White: not clean; possible loss of innocence; tainted; infectious.

Related Idioms: "White as snow," "White knights," "White lies," "White washed," "White magic," and "White collar."

Yellow: optimism; mental energy; intuition; cowardice (see also "Fire").

Gold: God; divine inspiration; reward.

Related Idioms: "Yellow-bellied," "Yellow fever," "Yellow tail," "Golden wedding," "Golden rule," "Gold digger," "Gold standard," and "Guild the lily."

COLORS

Color	Cultural Meaning	Personal Significance

Color	Cultural Meaning	Personal Significance

Color	Cultural Meaning	Personal Significance

Numbers

Numbers have always been regarded as having magical and mystical properties. Scientists, however, as well as other folks have varied attitudes about what numbers really mean to us. Some ridicule those who assign meaning to numbers whether as a function of numerology, astrology, or card reading. Others obsessively use numbers to make every decision, from whom they should marry to what breakfast cereal to eat. Balance, of course, is the prudent approach. We can look at the meanings of numbers in our dream symbol interpretation and transformation process, but using them to run our lives is not in our best interests. It is interesting to note that scientists will use numbers to crack all the codes of the physical universe and yet scoff at those of us who use numbers to crack the codes of the spiritual universe! I personally like what Cayce said about numbers, as quoted in Elsie Sechrist's *Dreams: Your Magic Mirror:*

Each individual vibrates to certain numbers according to his name, his birth date and his relationships to various activities. When numbers appear, they represent strength or weakness, assets or deterrents, change or stability. They are also signs or omens. They may be used as warnings or as aids in any manner helpful to the individual.[1]

As you acquaint yourself with the symbolic meaning of numbers, remember that each of us has his or her own perspective on numbers which always needs to be incorporated into one's dream processing work. We only mention the numbers from one to twelve in this glossary, but for an in-depth look at the Chaldean-Hebrew-cabalistic system of numerology (the system I believe is most correct universally), I highly recommend *Linda Goodman's Star Signs* (see Bibliography).

Universal Meanings:

One: When we think of the number one, we think of oneness of mind and oneness of power. One cannot be divided, so it refers to indivisibility and individuality. This is a number of strength. It is the basis for all numbers and represents a strong foundation, new beginning, creativity, Universal Force, and God. One represents a union with the Divine and a unity of humankind.

Step 1 on the program is where we admit and surrender in order to begin a new life: "We admitted we were powerless over _____ —that our lives had become unmanageable."

Two: This number is weaker than one. All even numbers are weaker than the odd because the odd numbers all contain a one, the unit of strength. Two denotes a beginning of the division of the Whole. It represents polarity, as in God and human, male and female, good and evil, higher and lower nature—all of which can signify balance. Two can represent a union or a pair, as in twins or marriage. Two is the number of sensitivity, balance, and parenthood.

Step 2 clarifies our realization that we can't recover as one, but need to pair up with a Power greater than ourselves: "Came to believe that a Power greater than ourselves could restore us to sanity."

Three: This number is a combination of three ones that become one again, as in the Father, Son, and Holy Spirit. Three stands for strength—the strength of spiritual conversion and conviction. In the dreamer it often represents the physical, mental/emotional, and spiritual self. It is the number of religion, idealism, hope, and

Divine Love. A dream with three in it almost always contains a message about the state of the spiritual condition of the dreamer.

Step 3 is when we merge into the one strength of our Higher Power: "Made a decision to turn our will and our lives over to the care of God, *as we understood Him.*"

Four: This is an earth number, a carnal number of materiality. Four represents the things of the planet and desires of the flesh. It depicts the elements of earth, air, fire, and water; four corners of the earth; and the four winds. It often means stability and balance on the earth plane, like the four legs of a table. It is the number of reason, equilibrium, materiality, desire, and earthly love.

Step 4 is where we examine our earthly vices to begin the process of stability and maturity in our lives: "Made a searching and fearless moral inventory of ourselves."

Five: Five represents activity. In a dream it usually means an immediate change of activity in its associations. It implies a reaching out to take things in hand and modify them. We work, create, build, and manipulate things with our hands which have five fingers. It is the number of movement, versatility, and written and oral expressions for change.

Step 5 is where we confess our past, creating a foundation for the biggest change ever to occur in our character: "Admitted to God, to ourselves, and to another human being the exact nature of our wrongs."

Six: Six illustrates the beauty and symmetry of all numbers. It is the number of unconditional love, as in the combining of two trinities. It denotes harmony and cessation of movement (the earth was completed in six days). Six is the number of our guides and teachers and symbolizes their love for us. The appearance of a six in a dream can refer to settling down in a loving union. It represents the feminine essence, compassion, love, and romance.

Step 6 is where we love ourselves enough to become willing to let God take our defects that will bring harmony to our personalities: "Were entirely ready to have God remove all these defects of character."

Seven: This is the number of our spiritual unity and transformation. God rested on the seventh day; there are seven spiritual centers (chakras) in humankind; there are seven candles on the Jewish candlestick; there are seven knots on Mohammed's golden rope. Seven announces a celestial influence and symbolizes a spiritual unit or mystical relationship. It represents the combination of Divine Love (three) with humanity's desires (four) leading to spirituality, healing power, universal love, and mysticism. It is the number of healing and transformation.

Step 7 is where we ask God to heal us: "Humbly asked Him to remove our shortcomings."

Eight: Eight can aggravate the materialism of four, causing the misuse of earth energy or vacillation in decisions. It also shows strength in the sense that it is a heavy karmic number and represents great burdens to overcome, by choice. It can lead to wisdom through discipline in harsh lessons learned on earth. It can also mean the beginning of a new cycle for the *final finish* (of lessons to learn). Laid on its side, an eight is the symbol for infinity.

In Step 8 we begin a list that will lead to the finish of the actions required to overcome the past: "Made a list of all persons we had harmed, and became willing to make amends to them all."

Nine: This number signifies the end of something. It is the termination of the natural order of things. Nine is the finish of a whole, as in death. It is the termination of whatever it is associated with, leading to a new order. It depicts the male essence—aggression, penetration, courage, and conflict.

In Step 9 we must make restitution for our past "sins," ending our relationship to the past and beginning a new order of our lives: "Made direct amends to such people wherever possible, except when to do so would injure them or others."

Ten: This is the culmination of numbers representing strength and a return to the one or the Godhead. It means perfection through a triumph over lessons and a return to a new beginning. Whereas nine is the death of the old and birth of a new order (death of the old relationship and birth of a new relationship or learning to live alone), ten is the completed cycle of the same basic order (completion of one part of a relationship: he had an affair, you're back together, and are renewing your vows). It's the culmination of a cycle that denotes a higher frequency of understanding either from good or from evil. The power of ten means rise and fall, love and hate, and can be used for good or evil. It is the number of triumph, leadership, and power.

In Step 10 we perfect our program by continuing to maintain vigiance in applying the principles in our lives: "Continued to take personal inventory and when we were wrong promptly admitted it."

Eleven: Although eleven can show the equality of individuality, side by side, it can also give the illusion of separation. Whereas two gives us a union, eleven represents a separating force, as in divorce, inability to see the other side, lack of empathy, or divided loyalties. Yet, as it stands with its own individuality, there can be worth on both sides. Eleven is considered the number of self-consciousness—where one sees self as singular yet joined to another. Eleven is sometimes seen as a higher expression of two.

In Step 11 we are asking to align our will side by side with God: "Sought through prayer and meditation to improve our conscious contact with God, *as we understood Him . . .* "

Twelve: This is a combination of forces that bring strength to the world to replenish it spiritually. It is the number of spiritual fulfillment and fruition. It is an expression of growth and number of congratulations from our guides, higher self, and the Divine. Twelve marks the time of ripening, when we become ready to reach out to others and create hope in them. There were twelve disciples (to carry the message of Christ and begin a new era) and twelve months to a year (then begin a new year). Twelve represents the fruition of hope and the planting of seeds to begin the cycle again. Twelve is never an ending nor beginning—it is a continuation of a cycle, as in the four seasons.

Step 12 is the culmination of our principles and asks us to use what we have gained to reach out and begin the process anew in others: "Having had a spiritual awakening as the result of these Steps, we tried to carry this message to (others), and to practice these principles in all our affairs."

Zero: The unconscious generally ignores zero when adding a sequence of numbers. However, when viewed as a circle, it often is used as a symbol for God, without beginning and without ending.

NUMBERS

Number	Cultural Meaning	Personal Significance

Animate Objects

(Domestic and Wild Animals, Birds, Marine Life, and Insects)

Domestic and Wild Animals

Animals are governed by the principles of life and death and can be as savage in their quest for survival as they are beautiful in the earth plane. In dreams, animals will take on the worst or the best of these characteristics, depending on the context of the dream and the attributes we personally associate with each creature. Animals usually represent our lower, physical nature and our primitive emotions. As a wild animal might represent our wild emotions and behaviors, the domestic animals represent our more tamed and disciplined selves.

Related Idioms: "Slimy as a snake," "Monkey business," "Dog days of summer," "Hungry as a bear," "Wolf in sheep's clothing," "Full of bull," "Bear down," "Take the bull by the horns," "The bark is worse than the bite," "Pig in a poke," "Monkey on the back," "Black sheep," "Don't look a gift horse in the mouth," "To get one's goat," "Let sleeping dogs lie," "To be on one's high horse," "To kiss till the cows come home," "S/he's squirrely," "Let the cat out of the bag," "Clever as a fox," "Wise as a serpent," and "Laughing like a hyena."

Universal Meanings: Bears (overbearing), bulls (stubbornness or deception), cats (independence), cows (eating disorders), deer (gentle nature), dinosaurs (old fears), dogs (faithful companion and unconditional love), donkeys (stubbornness or an ass), elephants (memory, great strength, or thick-skinned), goats (lasciviousness), gorillas (low-mental abilities or gangsters), horses (freedom or carrying burdens), lions (dangerous instincts), moles (hiding from the situation), monkeys (mischief), pigs (selfishness or gluttony), rabbits (fertility or promiscuity), rats (betrayal), reindeers (Christmas), sheep (the faithful or the follower), snakes (wisdom, evil, or temptation), squirrels (hoarding or hyperactive), tigers (they ate early Christians; see "lions"), toads (ugly behavior), turtle dove (fidelity, family values), unicorns (grace, purity, magic).

Birds

Birds are usually associated with mental activities, higher ideals, joy, happiness, and rising above the trials and tribulations of the world. But we have to use our common sense because, of course, chickens and vultures wouldn't be interpretated in the same way.

Related Idioms: "A bird in the hand is worth two in the bush," "It's the early bird that gets the worm," "Free as a bird," "Light as a feather," "Like a chicken with its head cut off," "Feather one's nest," "A feather in one's cap," "Dovetail," "Don't count your chickens before they hatch," "Chicken-hearted," and "Swan song."

Universal Meanings: Beaks (tendency to gossip or eating disorder), bluebirds (happiness or truthfulness), chickens (cowardice or stupidity), crows (death), doves (peace), eagles (freedom and keen sight), feathers (light-hearted), owls (wisdom or visit from the dead), parakeets (lovebirds), parrots (mimicking), peacocks (posturing), phoenix (rising from the ashes, immortality), ravens (God's promise to feed us; evil, to the readers of Edgar Allan Poe), robins (fresh and springlike), roosters (male cockiness), swans (beauty, grace, transformation).

Marine Life

The higher ideals of aquatic life would refer to the Christ Consciousness and seeking spirituality. The symbol of Christianity is a fish. However, aquatic creatures can also represent our emotional life with the cold-blooded features of sharks and alligators. There are also bottom feeders, such as catfish or bullheads, that would refer to our "feeding" off of garbage.

Related Idioms: "Happy as a clam," "Something's fishy," "Loan sharks," "Crocodile tears," "S/he's a cold fish," "Drink like a fish," "To fish for compliments," "To come out of one's shell," "Whale of a good time," "Groping like an octopus," and "A fish out of water."

Universal Meanings: Alligator (destructive emotions or a big mouth), clam (happy, as in a smile, or reference to the vagina), crocodile (see "alligator"), fish (sign for Christianity or cold-blooded), frogs (uncleanliness of body or speech or can turn into a prince), jellyfish (squeamishness or weak-willed), octopus (sexuality out of control), polywogs (undeveloped in spiritual matters), seahorse (playfulness), sharks (predators), shellfish (see "clam"), shells (life experiences from beauty to brokenness and ugliness), turtles (longevity), whale (overwhelming, smothering love).

Insects

Finally, we have insects. In dreams, they often represent irritations that "bug" us. They are pests that inflict us with disease and discomfort by stinging or biting. They can also, as with all symbols, refer to more pleasant things, such as fireflies, bees that pollinate, or the friendly ladybug.

Related Idioms: "Worm your way out of it," "Webs of deceit," "Fly in the ointment," "Get under my skin," "Beetle brow," "Bloodsucker," "To crawl into a cocoon," "The sting of words," and "To make the skin crawl."

Universal Meanings: Ants (activity, hard work), beetles (irritations), butterflies (metamorphoses of the 4th and 5th Steps), caterpillars (unrecognized potential), cobwebs (dull mentally), cockroaches (character defects), cocoons (gestating, protection), flies (see "beetles"), ladybugs (propriety), lice (uncleanliness), scorpions (sting of a bad situation or the situation will turn in on itself), spider (devouring attitudes), ticks (bloodsuckers), webs (getting caught in traps or deceit), worms (rotten).

Look for the characteristics that you associate with animate objects by correlating what element they live on (earth, air, or water), how they survive (predator, herbivore, cannibal, nocturnal, or diurnal), how they affect humans, their color(s), and any phonetic likeness to their name (lion = lying; alligator = I'll get her). Always include your personal attraction or repulsion to the beings in your interpretation equations.

ANIMATE OBJECTS

Symbol	Cultural Meaning	Personal Significance

Symbol	Cultural Meaning	Personal Significance

Symbol	Cultural Meaning	Personal Significance

Behavior and Activity

(Includes Sexual Dreams)

The positions, behavior, and activities of our dream images are all a part of the intricate understanding of the overall meaning of our dreams and visions. We must look for the qualities that embody the demeanor or action of the image. Just as standing up can refer to "stand up and be counted," smoking can mean our resolves "going up in smoke." People can meet a fork in the road depicting a choice to be made or they can find themselves sliding down a hill which is a warning of losing ground gained in previous progress.

Naturally, for program people, "slipping" can mean a return to addiction. Pregnancy usually means the gestation of ideals for a new life—in 12-Step programs this expresses the working of Steps 1 through 11. One of the most frequent questions asked about behavior in dreams is about sex and nakedness. To be naked usually refers to the exposure of ourselves or our feelings of vulnerability. Sexual intercourse in dreams can mean the union of masculine and feminine leading to a balanced self, or it may indicate a need to merge the characteristics of the person we are having sex with to our own. Sex in a dream can simply be a form of wish fulfillment. Debasing sexual acts can indicate the cheapening of our self. We must ask ourselves in interpreting positions, behavior, and activities: How does society view this? What is the play on words? How do I view this?

Related Idioms: "Chew on that thought," "Spare the rod and spoil the child," "Absence makes the heart grow fonder," "Tote that barge and lift that bale," "We'll cross that bridge when we get to it," "Shop 'till you drop," "Gentle's bet," "Don't do as I do, do as I say," "Don't cry over spilled milk," "Look before you leap," "Think before you speak," "Cut out that noise," "Dancing in the wind," "To draw and quarter," "Laughter is the best medicine," "To eat humble pie," "A cut above," "Don't get all hot and bothered," "Fall into the enemy's hands," "Fall in love," "Turn yourself around," "Shoot your mouth off," "Run away from your troubles," "All choked up," "Drowning in his sorrows," and "Eating his heart out."

Universal Meanings: Choking (unable to accept something), crying (warning of impending tragedy), cutting (get rid of something), dancing (celebrating, dance of life), diving (going into the past or unconscious), drawing (plan your next move), driving (if you are driving, you are in control of the situation; if another, he or she is in control), drowning (warning of heavy emotions or could be literal), dying (a change in consciousness), eating (usually literal or devouring something), falling (expressing an anxiety), fighting (warring with self or others), fishing (seeking the Divine), flying (indicates that you are astral traveling or soaring with high spiritual ideals), gambling (taking risks), giving birth (birth to new ideals), going below the ground (going into the past or the unconscious), going down (losing ground or losing control), going up (suggests that you are elevating your situation), handshake (meeting friends), killing (killing off the old and beginning the new), kissing (forgiving), laughing (don't take things so seriously), marrying (integration), moaning (unhappy with self), praying (beseeching God), sex (see second paragraph, p. 101), shooting (warring with unconscious or mouthiness), singing (flow of the Divine), sleeping (lack of awareness), stealing (taking something that is undeserved), suicide (killing off old attitudes, character, or life style), swimming (emotional activities), traveling (refers to the path you are on in life), wandering or going in circles (you are stuck in the same meaningless patterns).

BEHAVIOR AND ACTIVITY

Symbol	Cultural Meaning	Personal Significance

Clothes, Accessories, and Jewelry

Clothing

Clothing is something we use to protect ourselves from the elements, to signify our working positions, project our personal images to others, declare our ethnic affiliations, and even show what recreations we enjoy. Clothing plays just as diverse a role in our soul vocabulary, too. Our attire in a dream will help orient us to the direction of the dream's message: is it about our profession, play, religion, attitude, ego image, school, hobby, or something else?

The background of our dream in relation to the attire can be illuminating also. Do we fit in or is there something amiss? Is a piece of clothing too tight (restricting) or are we naked and exposed? Rich fabrics and beautiful colors can refer to reaping the reward of past actions, while soiled and dirty clothes can be referring to defects of character. Inappropriate dress may be drawing attention to incongruous images, actions, or thoughts that we need to examine.

Related Idioms: "The cloak and dagger," "Dress for success," "Wearing the pants in the family," "The naked truth," "From rags to riches," "Tied to his mother's apron strings," "Clotheshorse," "If the shoe fits," "Walk a mile in another's moccasins," "Nothing up my shirt-sleeve," "Skirt the issues," and "Stuffed shirt."

Universal Meanings: Coats (covering and hiding emotions or smothering love), dresses (attitudes about self and image to others), evening gowns (fantasies and romance), fabrics (the patterns and texture of one's life), jeans (genes or a rebellious attitude), nightgowns (sexual), pajamas (need for more sleep), pants (power in a relationship), raincoat (protect self from elements), seams (either binding together or coming apart), sexy clothing of any kind (seduction), shorts (coming up short), skirts (not facing something), sleeve (what's up it?), slips (losing the battle with something), suit (state of business), underwear (hidden attitude), uniforms (character symbolized by type of uniform).

Accessories

Accessories should be viewed not only by their color and condition but correlated to the body part that it supplements. Shoes often allude to our foundation (what we stand on), gloves to our work or duties (what we handle), and hats to our thought and attitudes (on our head). Purses hold our valuables, scarves protect our necks, and buttons hold things together.

Related Idioms: "Keep your head above water," "Keep your feet on the ground," "To face your troubles," "Don't stick your neck out," "Bee in your bonnet," "Handshake deal," "Head over heels in love," "The right hand doesn't know what the left hand is doing," "Slips through your fingers," "The hand that rocks the cradle," "Don't lose your head over it," "These boots are made for walking," "Cut off your nose to spite your face," "Giving handouts," "Button up your lip," and "Hats off to you."

Universal Meanings: Belt (holding things up or, if too tight, may refer to stomach problems), feet (firm foundation on something), fingers (pointing out something, reproach), glasses (examine the situation), gloves (protection from infections; see "hands"), hair (thoughts, red hair=temper, white hair=wisdom, gray hair=maturity), hands (take the situation in hand and change it; rough hands may indicate rough treatment of something or a helping hand; applause may be a sign of encouragement), hats (roles you play, thoughts), head (keep your head or use your head), purse (our valuables), shoes (firm foundation in something), tie (relates to business, sometimes uncomfortable pursuits), wallet (our valuables or identity).

Jewelry

Jewelry may be viewed as spiritual treasures or valuable attributes. A ring symbolizes a loyal union, while a necklace represents a union with God encircling us. A gift of jewelry can be referring to the treasure we may receive from another. When we give treasures in dreams, we might be referring to our generosity. We can also keep in mind the color of the stone and type of metal. Whereas gold and silver would refer to spiritual treasures, pot metal may be referring to the worthlessness of things bought with drug money. Most dreams with jewelry, treasures, gems, money, and precious metals are referring to our abundance, prosperity, and the valuable characteristics we are either acquiring or losing.

Related Idioms: "Being led around by a ring in the nose," "Sparkles like a gem," "Diamond in the rough," "Don't caste your pearls before swine," "Diamonds in the sky," "Blarney stone," "Crown of glory," "Fool's gold," "The family jewels," "Burns a hole in your pocket," "Don't take any wooden nickels," "A penny saved is a penny earned," "One person's trash is another's treasure," "Lucky charms," "A day late and a dollar short," and "All that glitters is not gold."

Universal Meanings: Amethyst (spiritual attributes), blue-white diamonds (divine influences, truth), bracelets (precious things you hold in your arms, like babies and family members), charms (sign of seeking protection or charming attribute), coins (something of value or consider costly to self), crowns (spiritual rewards and high spiritual thoughts), diamonds (eternal love), earrings (listen), emeralds (strength to heal, majestic), gold (God, high spiritual thoughts), ivory (purity), jade (healing and growth, often with Oriental overtones), money (see "coins"), necklaces (love of God), pearls (purity), rings (loyalty, faithfulness, love), ruby (deep love, used as fertility sign, majestic), silver (spiritual thoughts), treasures—buried (precious aspects of self not yet uncovered), wedding rings (union or integration with higher ideals).

CLOTHES, ACCESSORIES, AND JEWELRY

Symbol	Cultural Meaning	Personal Significance

Symbol	Cultural Meaning	Personal Significance

Figures and Features

Figures

We often hear the tenet that people in our dreams generally represent aspects of ourselves. Although this can be their purpose, it isn't necessarily their only one. For instance, strangers can represent aspects of ourselves (a robber can show what our behavior is robbing from us), but strangers can just as easily be someone we will meet in the future, an angel, or other spiritual guide. A shadow can be a fear from our past. Family members, friends, and co-workers can symbolize their dominant traits for us or their appearance can simply be informing us of something about *that* person.

Often, a figure in the beginning of a dream can be part of the anatomy of the dream, telling us when the origin of the problem started or with whom it started. For instance, my brother Chris (who often symbolizes the brother-Christ love for me), protecting me from my father at the bottom of the stairs, depicts my unconscious fear (basement) of people making fun of my spiritual beliefs (for example, Dad mocked me by saying that the ankh peace sign was the footprint of a chicken).

It is important to look for the professions of the figures in our dreams for a comprehensive view of the message they bring us. Are they authoritarian figures like policemen, judges, presidents, kings, or ministers, showing our need to petition a higher authority? Maybe they are in service work like a waitress, steward, or janitor, showing us the value of service. Maybe we see our mate as a movie star and this is guiding us to treat our loved one as the "star" of our life. Frequently, our guides talk to us from the image of some authority, helper figure, or other personage to emphasize the intent of their words or actions. Sometimes our higher self assumes these roles.

Related Idioms: "King of his castle," "Knight in shining armor," "Headless horseman," "Mother Nature," "Good witch of the North," "Mother of invention," "Soldier of fortune," "Father Time," "Nero fiddled while Rome burned," "Honor thy father and thy mother," "Children should be seen and not heard," "Prince of darkness," and "Angel of mercy."

Universal Meanings:

Authority Figures: Christ (Higher Power in us), God (ultimate source of all solutions), fathers (authority on earth plane), generals (in charge), judges (will evaluate us), kings (ultimate father on earth plane), police (disciplined behavior or thoughts), preachers (know right from wrong), presidents (in charge), priests (know sin and penitence), principles (disciplined behavior), queens (ultimate mother on earth plane), Solomon (wisdom).

Diversion Figures: Actors (playing a part), cartoon characters (life's not real), clowns (laugh a little more and don't be too serious), comedians (see "clowns"), drunks (need humility or out of control), gambler (taking risks), jesters (lighten up), jokers (a wild card in your life), politicians (don't count on the situation).

Divine Messengers: Aliens (universal knowledge), angels (divine communication), Christ (brings enlightenment), God (unconditional love), Mohammed (see "prophets"), prophets (speak for God), saints (speak of God).

Faithful Figures: Babies (birth of new ideal or consciousness), brothers (brotherly love), children (powerless or wondrous, immaturity), congregation (worship), fishermen (seeking things of the spirit), friends (a quality you see in yourself), hunters (seeking material things), pilgrims (seeking to worship), sisters (we're all children of God), students (seeking to learn).

Helper Figures: Construction workers (build up), cowboys (round up), doctors (correct defects), janitors (clean up messes), maids (service), mechanic (fix situations), postmen (communication), secretaries (keep track of things), servants (service), stewardesses (service with high ideals), tailors (bind things together), veterinarians (modify animal instincts), waiter or waitress (service).

Negative Figures: Convicts (wronging self or others), Nazis (repression), rapists (destroying purity or taking advantage), savages (aggressive behavior), shadows (fear of the unknown), slave (to passions), spies (scrutinizing for wrong reasons), terrorists (to terrorize self or others), thieves (robbing self or others), wardens (keep us imprisoned), witches (others gaining control of one's thoughts).

Nurturing Figures: Cooks (to feed the spirit), fishermen (seeking God), grandparents (soothe the emotions), mothers (comfort of life), nurses (soothe the soul).

Teaching Figures: Buddha (master teacher), detectives (to give more information), disciples (to teach Christ Consciousness, Indians (to teach about the earth), instructors (how to apply solutions), ministers (what is right and wrong), old people (our guides in dreams, maturity, wisdom), psychics (to instruct about past or future), scientists (to prove or disprove value of situation), sponsors (how to walk like we talk), teachers (information).

Protecting Figures: Attorneys (for defense), godparents (in spiritual matters), guardian angels (from danger), life guards (from emotions), parents (from childhood fears), police (for behavior), security guards (from negative influences), shepherd (from evil), soldiers (from negative influences), spirits (usually people from past who watch over us).

Features

Details of facial features, gestures, expressions, and voice inflections can be of as much value as race, creed, hair color, and clothing for interpretation of people in dreams. It is up to the dreamers to determine if they need to personally overcome the aspects illustrated by the gestures and facial features or if they need to provide help to someone else for these problems. Sometimes it is quite clearly a warning about the character of that person and telling the dreamer to be careful.

A big mouth can mean that you talk too much, while a smile can mean approval of your activities. If you are fighting with someone in a dream, it means that you need to improve relations with that person. Often, if you dream of a loved one in trouble, it is actually that loved one's psyche reaching out for help. When the dreamer sees a family member or friend die, it is usually talking about the death of that relationship—not the person him/herself.

Related Idioms: "Tongue wagging," "Hair raising," "Put on a happy face," "Wipe that look off your face," "Batting an eye," "Cut one's teeth on . . . " "If looks could kill," "If it had teeth, it'd bite you," "Truth is hard to swallow," "Don't get your nose out of joint," " Eye on the problem," "Keep your chin up," "Lose your head," "Nosing around," and "Two-faced."

Universal Meanings: False teeth (lies or gossip), fat (abundant, gluttony, hiding from self), flaw (shortcoming), frown (disapproval), ears (listen), eyes (watch), mask (façade to the world), nose (figure something out), nudity (exposed), pregnancy (gestation of new ideals), sharp teeth (sharp words), smile (approval), thin (needs nourishment of body, mind, or soul), third eye (spiritual sight).

FIGURES AND FEATURES

Symbol	Cultural Meaning	Personal Significance

Symbol	Cultural Meaning	Personal Significance

Plants

Plants, depending on the color, abundance, condition, and purpose, represent the quality of growth in our life. There is, of course, the tangled, unruly growth of jungles and vines that could depict a complicated state of mind or life as well as the well-tended gardens and pruned orchards that reflect our inner orderliness.

This symbol is so rich with analogies and comparisons to growth, bearing fruit, weeding things out, planting seeds, and pruning that most of the interpretation is self-evident. It is gratifying to see how plant life has been incorporated into our language and how easily we can extract a meaning. We have the "deflowering" of a girl, the "bloom" on the cheeks, "fruition" of a situation, "root" of a problem, and so on. When looking at flowers, we need to consider the traditional use for that flower, its color, and the context of the setting. For instance, a red rose can be a sign for Christ, a pink rose can be a sign of love or romance, and a white rose can be a symbol for baptism.

Related Idioms: "Out on a limb," "The concrete jungle," "Tree of life," Knock on wood," "Grow like a weed," "Turn over a new leaf," "You reap what you sow," "Clinging vine," "You are the apple of my eye," "Don't beat around the bush," "A rolling stone gathers no moss," "The grass is always greener on the other side," "Money doesn't grow on trees," "Family tree," and "You can't see the forest for the trees."

Universal Meanings: Branch (subsystem of something or attributes), bushes (proliferation), carnations (formal attitudes), fallen leaves (things to let go of), fertilizer (what's needed for growth is not always pleasant), fields (serenity), flowers (fruits of the spirit, celebrations, beauty, romance), forest (strength borne of maturity and experience, magical influences), fungus (unhealthy ideas), garden (fruits of your labor, reminder to tend to your growth, you reap what you sow), grass (marijuana or growth), harvest (deserved rewards), herbs (healing), jungles (unruly, out-of-control emotions), leaves (results of growth), lilacs (death), lilies (resurrection), limb (see "branch"), lotus blossom (higher self), moss (stagnant), nettles (sharp tongue), oak tree (strength), palms (relaxation or spiritual commitment), pine trees (everlasting life), plowing (prepare for growth), roots (foundation or source of situation), rose (Christ, love, romance), seeds (ideas), trees (the state of your family or spiritual growth), trunks (backbone), vines (many implications affecting situation), weeds (neglecting something), wilting (needs to meditate or other spiritual replenishment).

PLANTS

Symbol	Cultural Meaning	Personal Significance

Symbol	Cultural Meaning	Personal Significance

Health, Illness, and Death

In dealing with dreams that contain symbols of health, illness, and death we must first consider the literal possibilities. Health and illness dreams can give messages as simple as "eat more cranberries" to aid in cleaning the urethra, seeing yourself in an iron lung as a result of smoking, or seeing a funeral procession in front of you as you pull out from a bar as a warning about driving while intoxicated. A stopped-up toilet can be a warning about your bodily eliminations. Illness dreams can show an organ or area of the body being shriveled or mutilated as it might be affected by a disease. On the other hand, ulcerations, cysts, and cancers can symbolically depict our emotional or mental warring with ourselves. They can also mean that our defects are "eating us up."

People regularly have dreams that give definite instructions about how to heal themselves. A dream may apprise us to drink a certain tea, cut down on coffee, or cut out sweets. Alcoholics and other addicts repeatedly dream of being out of control with mind-affecting chemicals, making fools of themselves in public, having accidents in cars, and fighting. These are *literal* warnings to the dreamer who misuses and abuses drugs. People with eating disorders often have literal dreams about eating, ordering food in restaurants, and going to buy items in stores. These messages, too, often literally caution the person about needed changes in life style.

Dreams about death, however, seldom refer to death in the literal sense. The death of someone in a dream most often alludes to the death of that relationship. Our death can signify the death of our old attitudes and our consciousness making way for the new life. Dying is the transition from one state to another and denotes the ending of one form of consciousness and the awakening or birth of another. Dreams that are actually referring to death often come to us in metaphors in an attempt to ease us into the harsh reality. Impending death will sometimes be seen as attending a funeral, seeing a coffin, losing a tooth, black curtains fluttering, crossing an ocean or river, and wearing black.

Related Idioms: "He makes me want to puke," "Scared to death," "Starve a cold, feed a fever," "I died a thousand deaths," "Knocking at death's door," "He's a goner," "Healthy as a horse," "Gut wrenching," "Sick as a dog," "Break a leg," "Health, wealth, and happiness," "Dead as a doornail," "An apple a day keeps the doctor away," "Blind faith," "Paralyzed with fear," "Cough it up," "Sick to death of it," "That's a real gut rot," and "It gets on my nerves."

Universal Meanings: AIDS (wasting talents and knowledge or character defects destroying us), ambulance (urgency of matter), arm problems (need to care for others), blood (new life, warning about bloodshed or referring to the blood of the lamb), boils (toxic attitude inside person that will soon become apparent to others, unbecoming), cancer (being eaten up by something), constipation (need to let go or holding something back), convulsions (convulsive situation ahead), coughs (expel poisonous attitudes), cysts (see "boils"), diarrhea (warning against judging or condemning others, don't deplete self), feet problems (need to get yourself on a better foundation), hospitals (you need to fix something in yourself or with a relationship), injections (you need injection of something or warning about drugs), leg problems (see "feet problems"), lung problems (you need a breath of fresh air), mucus (infected poisonous situation, behavior, or thought), pain (warning), shots (see "injections"), sores (unbecoming anger at self or others), vomiting (see "coughs").

HEALTH, ILLNESS, AND DEATH

Symbol	Cultural Meaning	Personal Significance

Symbol	Cultural Meaning	Personal Significance

Inanimate Objects

(All "Things" Not Listed Elsewhere)

It is not difficult to translate the images in a dream if we quickly associate their *purpose* for us in life. Some are immediately self-evident, like salt which could mean the "salt of the earth" or a door being the way in or the way out of a place, situation, or behavior. A key is the key or solution to a problem, while a road is the path before us. Some symbols need a little more thought, such as plates, silverware, napkins, pots, and microwaves that we use for preparing, serving, or eating food, possibly meaning feeding our spirit or carnal appetites. Letters and newspapers contain information and are a way for our dreams to say, "Here is a message or some news for you." Pictures or mirrors are something to look at, leading us to the conclusion that we must look at ourselves or our situation more closely.

Begin to interpret the symbolic meaning of objects with a question, "What can I use this for?" A ladder is used for climbing—spiritually or socially. A fly swatter is used for getting rid of pests, a blender is used for blending—possibly meaning to blend your goals with that of your spouse—or an ax is used to separate something. A brick wall, roadblock, and closed door can denote barriers in a closed mind, the wrong path, a rigid attitude, or other impediment to growth. The purpose of the object, combined with the color, number, and context will often lead to a quick understanding of its symbology.

Related Idioms: "Born with a silver spoon in his mouth," "Milk of human kindness," "Hot dish," "Straight as an arrow," "Like a broken record," "Pillow talk," "Throw in the towel," "Don't burn your candle at both ends," "Life is a bowl of cherries," "Don't judge a book by its cover," "My cup runneth over," "That's like the pot calling the kettle black," "Bookworm," "A picture is worth a thousand words," "Don't pull the rug out from under you," "The pen is mightier than the sword," "Got it covered," and "Couch potato."

Universal Meanings: Alarm (warning), ax (separation), bathtub (clean up your act or body), beds (sex or need for relaxing), books (need for information), briefcase (business), broom (clean up something), camera (take a look at the situation), clock (numbers will clarify the message), couch (sloth), covers (hidden), diapers (babyish attitude that you make others responsible for), door (escape, the way out), food (consider literal message first, then look to see how the item is viewed; tomato=sexy, corn=corny, hot peppers= temper, fruitcake=crazy), fruit (see "food"; also homosexual, sweet, or fruits of the spirit), key (solution), knife (sexual innuendoes or cut it out), ladder (climbing), letters (message for you), mail (communication), mirrors (examine self), models (imitation of the real thing), news (new information), paper (clean slate), pen (communication), photo (see "TV"), plates (watch your diet), prescriptions (solutions to problems), scissors (cut it out or symbol of death), sink (see "bathtub"), soap (purity or need to clean up), suitcases (storing problems or resentments), tables (stability), telephone (see "letters"), tickets (opportunity or warning), tools (to build something), toys (need to play or playing around), TV (examine situation), vacuum cleaner (see "broom"), vegetables (see "food"; also dumb), walls (obstacle), washing machines (need for cleaning up image).

INANIMATE OBJECTS

Symbol	Cultural Meaning	Personal Significance

Spiritual Symbols

Religious symbols are highly personal and it is difficult to attach universal meanings to them. For instance, a cross can simply mean "to be cross," or refer to the "crosses" one bears in life, or signify love of Christ, or terror of hellfire and damnation. In the Russian Orthodox church a cross means a decision between morality or sin because of the additional slanted bar, situated below the first horizontal one, that points to heaven and hell. Spiritual symbols depend on our upbringing, our current religious affiliations, our concepts of a Higher Power, and progress along our spiritual path. Because of the sacredness and personal nature of spiritual symbols, we should never accept another's view of these nor impose our view of them on others.

For program people, some symbols will take on an additional spiritual meaning. Because so many meetings occur in church, that building not only can signify that a person needs more religious instruction but also that he or she needs more meetings. The "Good Book" could be referring to the word of God, the "Big Book" in AA, or the basic text of NA. Spiritual guides can manifest in the form of our sponsor or even Bill Wilson, the father of all the 12-Step programs.

Related Idioms: "Heaven help us," "Crosses to bear," "Dancing with the devil," "A snowball's chance in hell," "To fall from grace," "Nectar of the gods," "Sacred cow," "Hell's bells," "Hell hath no fury like a woman scorned," "A restless spirit," "Keep the faith," "Confession is good for the soul," "Pyramid power," "Confucius says . . . " "Out of spirits," "Stairway to heaven," "A ghost of a man," "The devil made me do it," "Scared the hell out of me," "Evil eye," and "The staff of life."

Universal Meanings: Angel (divine messenger), aura (indication of state of person you see it on—look up colors for clarification), baptism (birth of dedication to God principles), Bible (the word of the Divine), blessing (favor from Divine), Buddhist (master teacher), Christmas (birth of Christ Consciousness), church (need for more worship or religious instruction), cobra (wisdom), cross (long-suffering and sign of belief in Christ), crucifixion (unnecessary punishment of self), devil (tempter, blame), disciple (messenger from Christ), exorcism (do Steps 4 and 5), God (unconditional love, perfection, source, divine visitation), guru (teacher), heaven (reward), hell (punishment), Jesus (savior), Koran (see "Bible"), Mohammed (divine messenger), preacher (teacher), retreat (need for spiritual renewal), rosary (need for penance, Step 9), sacrifice (give up in order to get), saint (divine messenger), Satan (see "devil"), sphinx (mystical and occult secrets to be revealed), spirit (unknown part of self or messenger from other side), stairs (stairway to heaven or higher consciousness), Talmud (see "Bible"), Tower of Babel (you are not listening to God), umbilical cord (the silver cord that binds us to our body), virgin (untainted, inexperienced, to be sacrificed), Yin-Yang (whole unit composed of opposites, male and female, receptive and penetrating, negative and positive).

SPIRITUAL SYMBOLS

Symbol	Cultural Meaning	Personal Significance

Symbol	Cultural Meaning	Personal Significance

Vehicles and Buildings

Vehicles

Just as the body is our vehicle of conveyance through life, a vehicle usually represents our physical self going through life. An automobile is a frequent representation of our physical journey, but other conveyances are used by our subconscious to highlight various symbolic disclosures.

A boat can signify our voyage through life, an ambulance can warn of an emergency, a plane can refer to our spiritual journey, a barge can mean an overweight problem, while a bicycle can mean achieving balance. What we need to examine as we attempt to interpret is the color and condition of the vehicle: Is it red signifying a warning, does it have a flat tire suggesting that our support system is weak, or is it dirty and in need of washing? Are we driving the vehicle, which would denote having control of our life, or is someone else driving and, therefore, in control of our life? Are we going backward, forward, speeding, taking a back seat to someone, or broken down?

A dream of car trouble should first be viewed as a literal message about the actual cars we drive. Once the possibility of real car trouble is checked out, we should examine the dream as a message about our life or physical body. In interpreting vehicle dreams, we must always notice our intended destination. Are we going home, to work, on vacation, to the mountains, to the sea? Or maybe we're lost! Finally, the condition of the road is just as important as the vehicle itself and our destination. Is the road under construction, are there road-blocks, is it muddy, in good repair, and/or are there disturbing potholes?

Related Idioms: "Driving me crazy," "Spinning your wheels," "Smooth sailing," "Don't put the cart before the horse," "Don't give up the ship," "Train of thought," "Don't rock the boat," "Flying by the seat of your pants," "Batten down the hatches," "Like a pig on roller skates," "Tow the line," "Keep on trucking," "Flying high," "Up a creek without a paddle," and "Magic-carpet ride."

Universal Meanings: Ambulances (emergency situation), barges (overweight body), bicycles (balance), boats (emotional self, Christ holding one afloat), buses (overweight body, passengers can be aspects of self), caboose (past), canoe (go with the flow), cars (physical self), engines (power), gas (energy), gas tanks (stomach or uterus), gears (changing intentions), gear shifts (male genitals; see "gears"), glider (see "canoe"), hoods (façades), Mack trucks (overbearing), paddles (determination), passenger (not taking responsibility for self), planes (spiritual self, high ideals), speedometer (too slow or too fast in situation), steering wheels (willpower or control of one's life), transmissions (transition), tricycle ("unless ye be like a little child"), trucks (usually work, but same meaning as "car" if you drive one regularly), tugboats (one who diligently helps others), vans (the family), wheels (support system), wreck (warning, where self is headed if you continue with same course).

Buildings

While vehicles represent our journeying through life, buildings reflect the state or condition of our lives—mentally/emotionally, physically, and spiritually. The building is a reflection of what we have built in all three areas. The type of building can orient us to the aspect of our lives being addressed in the dream. Is this a dream about problems that began as a child (dream takes place in our childhood home), spiritual instruction (a church or temple), our future (a new house), our job (an office), our need to arrest a shortcoming (jailhouse), or a general need for help (in a hospital)? Each room will also give us some special emphasis of the message: the bedroom refers to sex or rest, the kitchen concerns nourishment, many beautiful rooms hint at our beautiful qualities, the basement depicts the subconscious or past, the bathroom means a need for better hygiene or cleaning up our act!

Related Idioms: "Window of opportunity," "Glass ceiling," "Jail bait," "S/he is the cornerstone of . . . ," "Blow your stack," "If you can't stand the heat, get out of the kitchen," "Open sesame," "A house made of straw," "Don't burn your bridges behind you," "Home sweet home," "A man's home is his castle," "Thick as a brick," "People who live in glass houses," "If these walls could talk," "A bridge over troubled waters," "Office politics," and "Bats in the belfry."

Universal Meanings: Attics (mind), basements (past activities or subconscious), bathrooms (need to clean up body or attitudes), beds (refers to sex or rest), bridges (crossing over to new situation, connecting divergent lives, or death), cafes (need to receive or give nourishment), chimneys (releasing things), churches (need spiritual instruction or need to worship), doors (the way in or out of a situation), factories (ability to fix or manufacture problems), foundations (support), hospital (need for correction), hotel/motel (temporary situation), houses (the state of being of self), kitchens (see "cafes"), library (research your options), living rooms (daily activities), offices (work), porch (your image to others), prisons (being confined by something), pyramids (mystery, initiation), schools (need to learn, lessons), stairs (up=future, down=past, up=higher consciousness, down=subconscious), stores (the cost of what you are doing), toilets (can refer to constipation or a "shitty" situation), towers (higher self), trailer (see "hotel"), tunnels (recesses of the mind), university (advanced lessons), warehouses (potential), windows (our view of others).

VEHICLES AND BUILDINGS

Symbol	Cultural Meaning	Personal Significance

Symbol	Cultural Meaning	Personal Significance

PART III

DREAMS FROM THE FELLOWSHIP

Dreams from the Fellowship

People can gradually become proficient at dream interpretation by simply doing regular dreamwork using the many good books available. However, it is advisable for program people to study dreams and visions directly from a program standpoint. Just like prayer and meditation, dreams and visions can help lead us to the spiritual growth we come to expect from our 12-Step programs. We can strengthen our spiritual principles, the recognition and the application of these, by communicating directly with our sleeping reality.

We will notice, as we begin applying these principles, that we can even help family members as they experience their own dream worlds. Don't think any age is too young, either. My brother and sister-in-law, Mike and Mary, learned that their twenty-four-month-old, Sheriden, was not too young to dream. One night,

Sheriden woke up screaming. Mike and Mary thought she was ill, so they walked and cuddled her, trying unsuccessfully to soothe the child. Finally, Sheriden looked up and frantically searched the room. She stuck her hands out as if pushing something away and cried, "Maw maw," which was her way of saying "monster." Both of them realized at that point that she'd had a nightmare. Up until then, Mike and Mary had thought she was too young to dream.

We will be able to better understand and help ourselves, our loved ones, and our fellow human beings, as we listen to and respond to the lessons and encouragement of our program through our dreams. One woman, Prudy E., from Washington State, put it this way:

> I love to hear newcomers, with only a short time clean and sober, bring up the topic of dreams at a meeting. It can be so fearful and confusing to the new people, just as it was to me. Today I just look at them and tell them, "Congratulations, I believe your Higher Power has kicked in and that, believe it our not, spiritual awakenings occur during our sleep." They usually look at me like I'm crazy but that's okay. One person said, "How can you have an awakening while you're asleep?" I haven't figured that one out, but I know it's true for me and I don't question it. God does work in mysterious ways.

Not only does God work in mysterious ways, but we know that many great adages are also paradoxes; for example, "You must give it away to keep it" and "You must surrender to be free" are common program sayings. So it needn't seem strange that one can "awaken" while one sleeps.

In this section, you will read about numerous spiritual experiences or "awakenings." Here we shall explore the personal 12-Step dreams of people from many different programs around the country and even the world. These dreams have been gathered by me over the course of three years during my consultations with recovery programs in the United States and Russia. They are the dreams, visions, and life events of my friends and family, both my biological family and my family among the fellowships.

The following vignettes were contributed by them as a form of 12-Step work so that we can all be enriched by their experiences with interpretation and transformation. Also I excerpted a significant number of these dreams from my personal journals. Since 1969, I have been synergistically combining and utilizing my dreams, the Edgar Cayce psychic material, and the 12-Step programs, all of which led to the development of this system of 12-Step dreamwork.

This system is rich and reliable for reaching tremendous heights of understanding about how to practice your principles in daily life. Basically it is offered as a forerunner for beginning your own dreamwork and an additional source for interpreting symbols and transforming messages that appear in your dreams. Whether you follow my system for dream processing with your 12-Step program or develop your own is not important. What is important is that you take advantage of this exciting opportunity to grow.

This section of the book provides various types of 12-Step dreams for your scrutiny and study. Each one is presented in light of the program. Each dreamer whose experience is included here worked with me to interpret the dream as it correlated to his or her program of spiritual growth and working the Steps.

The dreams are organized into ten categories. Six of those categories deal with general program goals and not directly with a specific Step. They are *Pre-program, Relapse, Reassurance, Humor, Death and Rebirth,* and *Precognitive and Warning.* In these dreams, we will correlate the message to their *purpose* in our program. The format for these dreams looks like this:

Context of the Dream:
Dream:
Interpretation:
Purpose:
Comment:

The other four categories of dreams deal directly with our Steps. They are *Examine Ourselves and Be Honest, Trust and Rely on God, Take Meritorious and Moral Action,* and *Service to Others.* In these 12-Step dreams, the content has been correlated with the objectives, principles, and Steps we were learning about at the time of the dream. The format looks like this:

Context of the Dream:
Dream:
Interpretation:

Objective(s):
Principle(s):
Step(s):
Comment:
It would be wonderful if we could gain in short order spiritual wholeness through our programs and dreamwork. But attaining wholeness is a process, not a destination; therefore, it's not realistic to think of a "completion" as our goal. You will be studying your dreams until the end of your life and continue to gain insight and strength for just as long. In answer to a question about how long a treatment would take to have an effect, Cayce answered:

A year or two years or seventy years—what's the difference! Is it building to use the time for constructive activities or for the gratification of self? If it is for the gratification of self, you'd better let it alone. If it is to be for constructive influences in the lives of others, begin. But begin by praying about it and making the promises—then do keep your promises to your Maker.[1]

The interpretations of the following dreams were done either by the dreamer, by the dreamer with my help, by myself, or as otherwise noted. Although I warn people not to take over the interpretation of others' dreams, in order to meet the goals of this book, I took the liberty of interpreting many of them to illustrate the process. In my 12-Step work, I will always interpret the first several dreams brought to me by people seeking insight. I then encourage them to do their own work and develop their own dream glossary and methods for understanding. If they continue to expect me to "do it for them," I quickly point out that just as I can't work their Steps for them, I can't work their dreams for them either. They soon get the idea and begin their own dreamwork.

As you read the following dreams, you will automatically begin to incorporate the method into your subconscious, and your dreams will accordingly begin to speak to you in a manner consistent with what we are doing in 12-Step dreamwork. You will be amazed at how quickly your dreams and your understanding of them will conform to this new way of looking at them.

In addition to imprinting the method into your subconscious, you may want to refer back to this section periodically to help clarify symbols and dream content that closely emulate your dreams. Each of the symbols in this section can be found in the index for easy reference or you can simply look up the general grouping where you feel that your dream fits and review that. Read them at random or in order. The experience of reading and seeing how the dreamer came to understand his or her dreams will be a tremendous help as you pursue your own dreamwork, your dreamwork glossary, and your dreamwork groups.

Pre-program Dreams

1. Allah, age 35, AA, one-and-a-half years in the program, Russia

Context of the Dream: I had this dream when I was only twenty-two and began using drugs.

> *Dream:*   I climbed mountains to the top and I saw a cross on the highest mountain peak. There was snow. My fellow travelers were around and I asked them to accompany me to the cross. Many were afraid and stayed behind. Many people saw us but wouldn't go. Only a few went with me. I said to my friend that the cross is the goal of our way. I understood that only I would make it alone. I saw it was my burden and my path.

Interpretation: Allah would work her way through a life that was leading toward God (cross on the mountain), even though her emotions for Christ were frozen at the time (snow there). She will want her fellow humans to go with her (fellow travelers), but only a few would find the way to the cross. She realized that our path to God is personal (alone).

Purpose: To prepare her for the future

Comment: Allah told me, "I awoke thinking it was not right because I didn't believe in God. I was an atheist. Sixteen years later, after two months on the program, I realized that my road *was* to God—the cross on the mountain." This was a precognitive dream for Allah, a young woman raised in a communist country who had no way to know what could transpire in her country and in herself. But her higher self knew what she was striving for. Frequently, climbing mountains will signify our striving for spiritual heights, the highest peak signifying seeking the most noble ideals and relationship to God. Water is the universal symbol for emotion and/or the spiritual well of life. Snow is frozen water and is a way for our subconscious to say that we are "cold" or "frozen" about something. So until the program of AA thawed her inner knowledge (none of which was possible until the fall of communism), Allah did not recognize what her inner longings were all about.

2. Sister of Allah, age 34, no program, Russia

Context of the Dream: Allah and her sister were studying yoga. Allah had been sober for one year in AA, and her sister dreamed this.

> *Dream:*   Allah lay dead in a coffin. She was in a red dress and, when I saw her, her cheeks were rosy, like she was alive. Then Allah flew up out of the coffin. She told everyone to come with her; it was better there.

Interpretation   (by Allah): Red is the color of a lower chakra. I believe my red dress signified the death of my lower nature, and I was released to fly to a higher level. This would be the AA program. I was finding my program to God.

> *Purpose:*   To show Allah and her sister what the spiritual path in a 12-Step program would do for them

Comment: This was a two-tiered dream. One interpretation was for Allah and the second was for Allah's sister, who originally had the dream. This is an excellent dream to illustrate the difference between interpreting the symbols and transforming the dream into a valuable life lesson. Allah would take the interpretation and transform the message into the reassurance she needed that what she was doing with the 12 Steps was right and that she was a good example for her sister. Allah's sister, however, would transform the same dream as a lesson about changing her own approach to life. I would venture to say that the sister's higher self was telling her that the 12 Steps were better suited for their circumstances than the yoga they were doing together. This dream was showing Allah's sister the benefits of killing off the old lower nature and going to the higher spiritual levels. It was the same dream and same symbol interpretation, but different transformations occurring in each of them.

3. Joe B., age 41, AA, five years in the program, Wisconsin

Context of the Dream: Before finding AA, Joe had been struggling with drinking for years and had decided he would never be able to quit.

Dream: I was sober and felt so good about myself.

Interpretation: Literal

Purpose: Showing him how wonderful sobriety will feel

Comment: Joe said, "I really thought that I had accumulated some sobriety when I woke up. I went around for about twenty minutes thinking I'd finally found sobriety and was so proud. Then I realized I was really still drinking and felt horrible." Like people who have relapse dreams when sober, people who are drinking can have sober dreams pointing them to a healthier life style. In Joe's case, it was a precognitive dream, for he truly did find sobriety within six months of this dream.

4. Michelle, age 30, AA and NA, nine years in the program, Colorado

Context of the Dream: Michelle had been trying to quit smoking by going through a hospital program. She tried hypnotism, acupuncture, repetition of positive statements, and tapering off. Nothing worked.

Dream: I am on another planet and the air isn't right for humans. I find it harder and harder to breathe. Finally, I end up in an iron lung.

Interpretation: I need to quit smoking!

Purpose: To show Michelle the effect on her body of the stress of smoking

Comment: This dream was five years before she actually quit, but very graphic about the difficulties her body was experiencing. Many dreams will situate us on different planets, in spaceships, or with aliens when our subconscious wants us to realize how strange or alien a condition is to us. The alien environment can suggest ominous overtones, like Michelle's dream in which she is warned that she can't survive in a hostile setting. More likely these images simply point out our unfamiliarity with the circumstances in which we find ourselves embroiled.

5. Robert H., age 31, in treatment, Indiana

Context of the Dream: Robert's dreams were turning to nightmares with increasing frequency.

Dream: I am riding my motorcycle down a hilly road. There are trees on both sides. All of a sudden my headlights go out, but I am still driving my bike. It is so black I can't see anything, then I wake up screaming.

Interpretation: Robert's path in life is very unstable (hilly road). The way he is running his life is leading to a blackout (headlights go out), but he is still operating in the dark (driving in a blackout).

Purpose: To let Robert know he may kill himself in a blackout if he keeps going in his addiction

Comment: This is a dream probably referring to the blackouts caused by his drinking and drug taking and the lack of light in his life. Roads and highways usually refer to the path we are taking in our lives. The road can be under construction, for instance, indicating that a new way is being prepared for us. Often we will see a roadblock that indicates either we should not continue living the way we are or that something in our lives is preventing us from advancing. The condition of the road is usually the condition of circumstances in our life.

6. Unknown woman (taken from *Dreams: Your Magic Mirror*[2])

Context of the Dream: The dreamer's husband had recently begun to drink too much.

Dream: I dreamed I saw my husband with a cocktail in his hand. His head was wobbling unsteadily because his throat had been cut from ear to ear. I wasn't horrified at the sight because there was no blood to be seen.

Interpretation (by Elsie Sechrist): "The dream was clearly telling her to use her influence to help him overcome this tendency (to drink to excess). It indicated quite literally that he was beginning to lose his head over liquor."

Purpose: So the wife could influence her husband to more healthy pursuits

Comment: It is interesting to note that she could see no blood. We often say in the program that if someone were cut, we wouldn't hesitate to help, but with addiction there's no blood, so we don't recognize the help the person needs. Typically when our dreams show grotesque sights of blood and guts, deformities, and nauseous wounds, these are graphic techniques our subconscious uses for getting messages across: "You're losing your head" or "Cut it out!" or "This situation is a bloody mess." The more gruesome the scene, the more determined the higher self is that you understand the intent of the communication.

7. Carol Ann, age 36, CA and Recovering Couples Group, ten years in the program, Colorado

Context of the Dream: I had been going to Coda but had not yet admitted I was a drug addict. My addiction was increasingly more serious and my life was a mess.

> *Dream:* I was in an incredibly black room with a door behind me. In front of me was the whitest ice skate I have ever seen. It had a cold steely blade.

Interpretation: She was skating with death (black room). She knew the way out from something in the past (door behind her represented the 12-Step programs she learned about in Coda). Her whole attention was on cocaine (incredibly white skate) and cutting herself in on it (steely blade). Since skates usually come in pairs, the absence of one would indicate that someone she knew who also used drugs was going to be cut out of her life.

> *Purpose:* To awaken Carol Ann to the fact that she was close to death

Comment: Carol told me, "A few days after this dream my friend Bobby C. died of a cocaine overdose. I know the blackness, the white skate, and the blade were a warning about Bobby's cocaine overdose. A few months later I found the program." What Carol didn't immediately realize was that she would have been dead shortly if she hadn't found the door. One skate had already been lost to darkness and she was soon to follow. Although white is usually a color that connotes purity of thought, innocence, and celestial things, for addicts it takes on an added dimension. White is the color of cocaine, speed, heroin. Any white powdery substance in the dreams of addicts must routinely be viewed as a possible symbol for drugs.

8. C. F., age 23, AA, NA, and Coda, five years in the program, California

Context of the Dream: C.F. was in high school and out of control with drug use, even as a freshman. He had this recurring dream.

Dream: I am really wasted on pot and alcohol and driving my Dad's BMW on a deserted road. I crash into a ditch and am not hurt, but am worried what my dad will say.

Interpretation: Like so many of my dreams this one came true, the only difference was that I was not high at the time. In fact, I was in and out of NA at the time.

Purpose: To prepare him for the consequences of his dangerous driving habits

Comment: This dream was not only precognitive, as C.F. correctly interpreted, but was a warning from his higher self that his addiction was leading to a "crash." His using got so out of control in high school that he was finally admitted into treatment before graduation. C.F. often has precognitive dreams and has to pay special attention so that he can take preventative measures when the guidance comes to him.

Examine Ourselves and Be Honest

(Steps 1, 4, 8, and 10)

9. Daniel C., age 45, Coda, two-and-a-half years in the program, Virginia

Context of the Dream: I was not active in the program at this time.

Dream: A huge, evil, powerful man confronts me. I am in a narrow room. There is no exit. There is no escape. It is possible I could fight my way past him. Now he has his assistants, at least three of them around him. They wrap a rolled-up towel each around him at different levels and pull it tight, like around his neck, chest, stomach. Now the stress of this tightening causes him to turn on his powers. He grows bigger, wider, more evil. He is so powerful and I cannot possibly fight, can't escape. I am terrified. Hopeless. I see that two heads and two snakes are growing out of his neck.

Interpretation: Dan's life is very narrow (narrow room) and his defects (evil man) are closing in. At first he could work out his problems with the program (possible to fight his way out), but Dan's many defects (many towels) and his twisting of things (wrapping or twisting the towels) are increasing (assistants appear). Dan is two-faced (two heads) and says venomous things about others (snakes coming from neck). The stress caused by his defects only serves to make them worse (the monster grows stronger as the towels tighten). He is powerless over his character defects.

Objective(s):   Be honest

Principle(s):   Powerlessness

Step(s): 1

Comment: This dream is a 1st-Step dream because Dan is being asked to face his powerlessness so that he can really get into the program and be active. Although we don't have enough information about Dan to get very specific about all of the defects (only Dan knows for sure), this dream does give us an extraordinary amount of information. He has a tendency to be two-faced and say sharp things about others. The reference to his chest and stomach are pointing out other areas where shortcomings are constricting him and getting worse. Daniel might have problems in romance (chest=heart) and in gluttony (stomach). We could even extrapolate further and wonder if the towels (something normally used for wiping up) don't signify his need to clean up these problems. Only Daniel could get to the exact meaning of each of the symbols, but the warning is clear—get back to your program and "throw in the towel!"

10. Gary C., age 42, AA and NA, nine years in the program, Indiana

Context of the Dream: I have nine years of being clean and sober, and it has been brutal at times. My dad died last year, my mom died this year, my wife has breast cancer, and I have glaucoma.

> *Dream:*   I was driving down the road and was real depressed and could end it right there. Then I realized that was not the solution. I wasn't beyond asking for help. But I realized my help was in Wisconsin, so I'd have to move up there because therapy would be a long time.

Interpretation: Mostly literal

Objective(s):   Examine self and be honest

Principle(s):   Admission and surrender

Step(s): 1

Comment: Gary said about his dream, "My wife got a call from our past therapist up in Wisconsin only two days after this dream.

The therapist had a dream about my depression! This confirmed that I would go for help if I get in trouble." When other people have dreams that coincide with ours, it is emphasizing and confirming its importance to us. Gary had been in therapy years earlier in Wisconsin, which is "above" his state of Indiana. This doesn't necessarily mean that he has to move to Wisconsin, but it could be a message about the "elevated" thinking in choosing therapy over suicide.

11. Anonymous woman, age 24, AA, four years in the program, North Carolina

Context of the Dream: She had been struggling with a more in-depth approach to her 4th Step (and 10th).

> *Dream:*   I was washing the car I used to drive before I was sober. The time of the vacuum ran out before I was done with the outside. Then it changed into my lover's car and I started cleaning the inside. The time also ran out, but I found four to five quarters more to continue with the inside.
>
> I was walking through a stream, parts were a foot deep and other parts only inches. I was aware that there may be water moccasins along the way and proceeded with caution. The appearance of the numbers two, four, and ten echoed through my dreams.
>
> Finally the image of the ocean appeared and the feeling was that of safety, relief, and jubilance. Connection to the earth in a very emotional (dancelike) context.

Interpretation: I see the car as my consciousness with my focus on "cleaning house." I see the change in vehicles as a recognition of a change in my support system (from drinking world to sober world) followed by a change in focus (exterior to interior). Water represents emotion to me, and walking cautiously through the stream while aware there may be "snakes" reminds me of my inventory taking. I continue to walk my path (upstream) steadily with faith in spite of the danger. The repetition of two, four, and ten reflects both "coming to believe" in a Higher Power (Step 2 represented by the ocean) and taking an honest and thorough inventory as well as a daily one.

> *Objective(s):*   Examine self and be honest; trust and rely on God

Principle(s):   Honesty, self-examination, trust, hope

   Step(s): 2, 4, 10

Comment: It is fascinating that this dream actually gave her the numbers of the Steps her dream was referring to. The four to five quarters were also referring to the 4th and 5th Steps of "cleaning house." Water usually represents emotion, a need for cleansing, or it can refer to Jesus and baptism. Because all life sprang from the ocean, ocean dreams can refer to God or the power of God, as it did in her dream. The snakes, of course, were referring to the dangers and temptations she might face as she wades through the emotions while working the 4th and 5th Steps.

12. Nona, age 61, Alanon, newcomer, Siberia

Context of the Dream: Nona had been to only two Alanon meetings when her husband came home one evening and untypically gave her flowers as a gift of appreciation. Her husband explained that he did this because she loved him and treated him as an equal despite his problems.

   Dream: There was thunder and lightning and Mother Mary stood before me dressed in white. I touched the silver chain my husband presented me. I was surprised that I hadn't noticed the medallion there before. There were bright stones all around it. (Suddenly my eyes were open; this part wasn't a dream. Then I continued dreaming.) Mother Mary never said anything, but I cried out, "I see you and I believe you are here." She melted into silver. Then I went back to the room where we were watching TV, and someone had taken my seat which was the best position in the house. My purse was scattered in dust with money lying around. I understood that these things were not important.

Interpretation: The thunder and lightning and Mother Mary's presence was a contact from the Divine for Nona (melted into silver). She had felt chained (silver chain) to her husband, but it was her gift (medallion with bright stones) that she had never realized before. She is being given information (TV) that a high position (good seat) in life and money (purse in dust) are not the important things in life.

   Objective(s):   Examine self and be honest; trust and rely on God

Principle(s):   Analyzation, guidance, love

   Step(s): 3 and 4

Comment: This dream was reinforcing the new principles she was learning from Alanon. An actual visitation from the Divine occurred, announced by the thunder and lightning. Mother Mary's presence was enough to illustrate the celestial nature of the message, but Nona's guides wanted her to know the extreme value of the visitation by having her melt into silver. Since silver is also a symbol of the Christ Consciousness and enlightenment, it was only highlighting the importance of her vision.

13. Drew, age 44, AA and NA, twelve years in the program, Canada

Context of the Dream: Drew had these dreams during the first year of his clean and sober time. They contained a recurrent theme.

   Dream: Character defects would come on placards in six-inch letters. They flew at me into my face—jealousy, dishonesty, intolerance.

Interpretation: Examine your character defects and look at them with love for yourself (six is the number of love).

   Objective(s):   Examination of self

Principle(s):   Honesty

   Step(s): 4

Comment: Notice the additional meaning of "in your face" with the defects flying at him. Sometimes the smallest snatches of dreams contain a tremendous amount of information. No matter how insignificant a dream or partial dream appears at first, we must promise ourselves to record it all. Many times the meanings become clearer long after we had the dream. I've had the experience of having dreams or seemingly meaningless details take on a clarity years later and be of benefit to me at that time.

14. Olya K., age 27, AA, NA, and OA, two years in the program, Russia

Context of the Dream: At seven months' sobriety, I had disagreed with my roommate about her having a friend over whom I didn't like. I told her strongly that he wasn't a good person and railed at her about it. That night I had this dream.

   Dream: I had warts all over my head and body. I was so frightened and it was so ugly. I went to my roommate, also clean in NA, and asked her what was wrong.

Interpretation: The warts were my anger and lousy behavior toward my roommate.

Objective(s): Examine self and be honest; take meritorious and moral action

Principle(s): Self-examination, courage

Step(s): 4 and 10

Comment: Olya has a difficult time controlling her anger and condemnation of others. This dream was showing her just what it looked like to act that way. A common way of expressing our unbecoming behavior will be with warts, pimples, tumors, and disfigurements. They are "ugly growths" that are shown to the world—in other words, our images and behaviors with others are growing worse and are ugly to boot. Pimples, cysts, and boils often refer to emotions we have infecting us inside which may erupt soon. Sometimes our mouths are deformed, referring to our ugly, mouthy actions, or our nose will be shaped like a pig's, illustrating our hogging the attention for something. If these things appear clearly on our bodies, then we have the added dimension to the message that whatever the problem is, it's already pretty obvious to everyone else!

15. Shelly, age 45, AA, NA, and ACOA, twenty-four years in the program, Alaska

Context of the Dream: I was working in Russia and knew that it was easy to get a degree from Moscow University, maybe by buying off an official or doing only a fraction of the work necessary. I was going to ask the president of the organization I worked for to check into it for me.

Dream: There was a plump girl in a blue party dress. They were supposed to get a guardian for her and the girl could pick her out. She sat at a board table and saw a picture of woman who looked like herself, but grown up. That's who she picked. It was I. I took the girl to my brother's and we drove around with his kids. Then the girl wanted her diploma from the school even though she hadn't been attending. I tried to get it for her, but they didn't want to give it. I wondered if it was such a good idea.

Interpretation: The girl is I. I am plump with the abundance of my Father in heaven (blue dress). I pick my higher self to look out after me (guardian who looks like me). My brother is known for being indulgent with his kids, which I was being with myself. I did not work for the diploma and did not deserve it.

Objective(s): Examine self and be honest

Principle(s): Consistency, integrity

Step(s): 10

Comment: When we see others in our dreams, they can represent the qualities that we attribute to them in real life. They illustrate that aspect of ourselves; thus my brother stood in for my indulgences of my immature wishes. There are many times, however, when people in our dreams simply represent themselves and our interaction with them. As we get to know our dreams, the difference will soon be apparent how the figures in our dreams present themselves. We will come to know if certain figures mean an aspect of ourselves, a quality in general, or if they are literally playing the part of themselves.

16. Raymond, age 45, NA, ten years in the program, Utah

Context of the Dream: Raymond is a natural Gypsy type and relocates a lot—not because of any problems, he just likes the life style. He decided to finally straighten out his difficulties with the IRS that began during his addiction and continued because of his Gypsy life style.

Dream: I started working on a new construction job. The foreman and I had an argument about the work he wanted me to do. He felt that I should know how to do it, but I told him I hadn't been trained for it. I'd also taken another job, which I was supposed to begin at 1:00 p.m. I needed to leave by noon to get to it and I had to tell my new foreman about leaving. There was some anxiety, but then I realized that I needed to make a choice between the two. On the job I'd already started one of the men told me he knew how to keep his entire check and would let me in on his secret. I had a momentary temptation to do the same, but then decided to go straight with the IRS. I needed to be honest because it helped me to feel better about myself.

Interpretation: Raymond needs to build his life (construction) anew, but feels he hasn't had the proper training although his higher self says he has (foreman). He should complete past lessons (noon) before beginning new ones (1:00). Raymond needs to be honest about his choices in life (tell foreman) and honest with the government (changing jobs frequently and cheating the IRS) so that he can feel good about himself.

Objective(s): Examine self and be honest

Principle(s): Courage

Step(s): 8

Comment: Raymond was reaching a higher level of spiritual understanding in his program. He realized that it isn't just individuals in our life that we need to be honest with, but companies and government bodies also. It was not only necessary to make amends and clean up his act with the IRS, but also to those he had worked for and whom he may have caused problems for due to his constant here-again, there-again life style. The reference to time are numbers with a clear message in the lesson of the dream. Twelve (noon) is the number of completion of a cycle, enabling us to begin a new one in the same order. In other words, he had worked the program on the personal side of his life with friends and family and done a good job. It was now time to start over (one o'clock, the number of beginnings) and begin the process again in working the 12 Steps in the business aspects of his life.

17. Prudy E., age 42, AA and NA, three years in the program, Idaho

Context of the Dream: I had become such a selfish, self-centered person during my addiction and was working on that particular part of my program when I had this dream.

Dream: I was in Colombia and found myself in a boat going down a canal that would normally be a street. There were sidewalks on either side. I had all the dope I could want in my lap, and my husband and others stood on the sidewalks of the canal unable to get to me. I had it all to myself. I was holding this dope up and laughing at my husband because he couldn't reach me and couldn't have any.

Interpretation: Just as in her using/addictive days (in Colombia with dope), Prudy is going on an emotional path by herself (alone in boat). She is isolated from her husband and friends (they can't reach her from the side) and she is not concerned with her husband's feelings (laughing at him).

Objective(s):   Examine self and be honest

Principle(s):   Self-analyzation

Step(s): 4

Comment: Prudy said, "I'll never forget the intensity of that dream and how it made me look at myself. I know God was speaking to me through that dream, showing me what I had become, thus aiding me in that particular area of my recovery." For drug addicts, dreams about South America are part of the anatomy of that dream, indicating that the problems addressed in the dream originated with their drug abuse.

Trust and Rely on God

(Steps 2, 3, 6, and 11)

18. Steve, age 40, Coda and Alanon, newcomer, Wisconsin

Context of the Dream: My wife, Bunnie, is a sober alcoholic and we've had a lot of problems. Recently she came home after a separation, but I lost my driver's license so she has had to drive me everywhere.

> *Dream:*   Bunnie and I are in our car. She gets out to do something and I know I'm not supposed to drive, so I start the car and get out and expect the car to follow me. I take off and look back and the car has gone the other way. I am amazed that it goes in and out of other cars, but doesn't hit anything. Finally it gets to a busy intersection and crashes. Police come, and I catch up to find a minister's son behind the wheel. I blame the accident on the minister's son.

Interpretation: Although Steve feels he is not in control (not driving), he still is running on self-will (expects the car to follow him). This will lead to a crash in his life. Higher authorities (police) come to take care of it, and Steve realizes that his higher self (minister's son) is in charge. He blames God for his predicament (the minister's son also represents his immature attitude toward God and religion).

Objective(s):   Trust and rely on God

Principle(s): Acknowledgment of position

Step(s): 2

Comment: This dream is showing Steve that his will is opposed to God's will and that he is out of control and headed for a crash. He needs to acknowledge that he isn't thinking straight and isn't in charge. He is blaming God for what he himself has started. As stated earlier, vehicles usually represent our journey through life, and the driver will establish who is in control of the situation we are dreaming about. In this dream Steve wasn't in control of his life and he wouldn't let his wife be either. He is seeking some sort of spiritual help, but is not integrated in his path because one part of him goes one way and the other, another. The "minister" is obviously referring to religion—but the son mirrors the immature nature of his religious ideas. Images of children will often refer to the past, immaturity, or youthful thoughts. So this is a direct reference to this man's immature religious ideas that are dividing his path as an adult.

19. Helen R., age 33, AA, seven months in the program, Russia

Context of the Dream: My grandmother was a Christian in communist Russia. I barely knew this grandmother who died when I was young.

Dream: Grandmother appeared to me and gave me a gift to keep. It was a cross on a chain, and there was one pearl that moved freely on the chain toward or away from the cross.

Interpretation: The cross is her new-found freedom in a Higher Power that Helen calls Christ. The pearl represents herself and her cleansing from addiction. She is free to move toward or away from her Higher Power, but she is always connected.

Objective(s): Trust and rely on God

Principle(s): Hope

Step(s): 2

Comment: We say in AA that if the program chases you away, the booze will bring you back. Helen is being told that even if she "slips" or moves away, she is always connected to her Higher Power. This is her hope and faith for the future. Gems, as well as coins, money, gold, and silver, frequently pertain to the spiritual treasures we are given. They demonstrate the value we will receive from practicing the principles. Sometimes we will find treasures under floorboards or buried somewhere. This means we are standing on firm spiritual footing. If they are found in the basement, that could indicate that we received good religious training in our childhood. If an old person gives us jewels or treasures, it ordinarily means that one of our guides is helping us find our way back to God. In Helen's dream, her grandmother was the family legacy to Christianity that was repressed through communism but reborn again in the granddaughter. The grandmother was probably helping Helen from the other side.

20. Anne, age 39, AA and OA, fourteen years in the program, Washington, D.C.

Context of the Dream: I was having a particularly hard time with my OA program and kept going to my old, sick eating habits. I had a new child and there were pressures at my job. I was having a rocky time.

> *Dream:*   Someone from school had a party at a beautiful house and I was jealous. I decided that the party I planned for Christmas would never do because my house was not as nice. A guy and I went up to the second floor and began playing a piano. I overheard people talking downstairs. They said awful things about me. I walked halfway down, leaning over the banister and began defending myself. The hostess said I had ruined the party and ruined her life. I kept defending myself.

Interpretation: Anne is learning (school) about her body image. She is envious of others' looks (beautiful house). She is ashamed of her own looks (her house is not as nice) and unable to celebrate Christ in her life (can't give Christmas party). Her solution is to raise to a higher level (second floor) and bring harmony to her life (play the piano) and balance her inner self (male aspect of her). Her past failures (you ruined the party) keep undermining her confidence (badmouthing her), but she doesn't completely revert back (only halfway) and defends her growth.

> *Objective(s):*   Trust and rely on God

Principle(s):   Hope, restoration

> *Step(s):* 2

Comment: Anne was having a tough time with her eating and consequently her body image. She also had trouble believing she could trust God to restore her to eating sanity. Playing instruments usually refers to the harmony in one's life. If we are female and dream of a man or vice versa, it is usually referring to the masculine part of our femininity or the feminine part of our masculinity—as in the Yin and the Yang, suggesting balance. Stairs and ladders reflect our path to higher ideals or our lower, more human countenance. If we traipse below ground level, it generally means we are going into our past (childhood or past lives) or that we are delving into our subconscious.

21. Drew, age 44, AA and NA, twelve years in the program, Canada

Context of the Vision: I was told to do my 3rd Step in treatment. I went to my sponsor's room and was angry. "How dare they tell me to work my 3rd Step," I thought. "After all, I'd already had a blue/white light experience." I was so angry that I blacked out. That scared me. I got down on my knees and said, "I don't care what happens if I die or go insane, I give up." Then I had a vision and out-of-body experience.

Vision/Out-of-Body Experience: I went out into the universe. I wanted to look back toward earth, but realized I could see all. It was the first time I became aware of "I AM." I knew I could go on. I could see in all directions, be in all directions. I knew I could go farther, but realized it wasn't time and came back.

Interpretation: A spiritual experience.

Objective(s): Trust and rely on God

Principle(s): Surrender, love

Step(s): 2 and 3

Comment: Drew said of this experience, "When I woke up, I knew I'd found who I was." This type of spiritual experience happens to about one-third of people who really work their 12-Step program and is akin to the spiritual awakening of Bill Wilson when he found his sobriety. Many folks worry that they don't have a flash of lightning-and-thunder type of experience to mark their conversion into this higher state of consciousness. Just because we may have a series of gradual awakenings instead of a huge thunderous one does not take away from the importance or validation of the changes in us. It is my suggestion that if this type of thing bothers us, we must ask our dreams to give us the explanation. We never again have to be bothered about these types of questions if we remember that our subconscious and our helpers from other realms *want* to answer our questions. All we need do is ask.

22. Sue, age 42, S-anon, one year in the program, Virginia

Context of the Dream: My husband and I were separated and I was in a lot of pain. My mother-in-law, who hadn't much liked me before, was actually in my corner during this time.

> *Dream:*   My mother-in-law, my husband, my daughter, and I were visiting an amusement park. I said that I didn't want to ride the roller coaster, because I had ridden it before and I was afraid. I looked around and we were already on the roller coaster, with my mother-in-law by my side, and I thought to myself, "I will live to get off this roller coaster, because I've ridden it before. If I shut my eyes it won't be so scary." I knew I would live to get off even though I was afraid.

Interpretation: Sue was terrified of the horrible emotional ups and downs (roller coaster) of separation from her husband. Not only Sue but her husband, mother-in-law, and daughter were also experiencing the same thing (on the ride with her). Her mother-in-law was a source of support (at her side). If she would have blind faith (close her eyes), she would be fine.

> *Objective(s):*   Trust and rely on God

Principle(s):   Faith

> *Step(s):* 3

Comment: Emotions are often symbolized as waves in the ocean, currents in the river, downpours, tempests, or frightening rides such as Sue's roller coaster. Raging emotions can also be characterized as runaway trains or other vehicles, wild snarling animals, and forest fires. Repressed emotions will come to us as volcanoes, pimples and cysts, and bombs.

23. Lin, age 51, Coda, six years in the program, Virginia

Context of the Dream: Lin had a number of severe stresses in her life with a divorce, losing a job, making a major move, and finally facing some incest issues from her childhood.

Dream: There is a baby with a mustache lying on the stairs on the third step.

Interpretation: Her new life (baby) and wisdom (mustache) lay with the working of the 3rd Step.

Objective(s): Trust and rely on God

Principle(s): Surrender

Step(s): 3

Comment: The beauty of this kind of dream is its simplicity and directness. Dreams and visions of babies who can talk are particularly beautiful; if they look older than their years (like the mustache above), it can signify a birth of a new consciousness and/or spiritual ideals. Babies and children are not interchangeable in our symbolic language. Whereas babies represent new ideals and the birth of a higher consciousness, children often represent things from our childhood or immature attitudes and actions. Babies are also our creative projects. Frequently the babies in my dreams portray my work, usually books.

24. Sharon S., age 37, ACDF, Coda, and S-Anon, two years in the program, Virginia

Context of the Dream: I had been in the programs for one-and-a-half years and had some trouble feeling my feelings.

Dream: I was standing in the ocean and waves kept crashing over my head. I was terribly frightened because I could not move and thought I was going to drown. Diane, my friend from one of my 12-Step groups, was standing at the water's edge telling me, "It is okay. You need to experience it and it will not hurt you." I then stayed in the water and it was okay.

Interpretation: The waves are my emotions, and I need to feel them and experience them in order to get well.

Objective(s): Trust and rely on God

Principle(s): Surrender

Step(s): 3

Comment: People from dysfunctional families will have trouble feeling their emotions. Before we get to the point where we are capable of feeling our emotions, we may have dreams of snow (frozen emotion) or frozen ponds and lakes. Once we reach a place where we begin to feel emotions, we have dreams of waves crashing over us, downpours, and drowning. Specific emotions are generally represented by specific objects or animals, while a general emotional state is represented by the elements of the earth. What we do in the dream to get out of or accept these situations will be our answer to the plight. Sharon's solution was to relax and just experience her emotions.

25. G. G., age 64, AA and OA, twenty-five years in the program, California

Context of the Dream: I had seventeen years' sobriety and had reached a point where I didn't want to "miss the mark" any more.

Dream: I was dancing with the devil (living with, pushing away) and dancing with him. Finally I realized I didn't want or need him and told him to go.

Interpretation: G.G. no longer wanted to mess around with her defects (the devil in her) and told him to go.

Objective(s): Trust and rely on God

Principle(s): Willingness

Step(s): 6

Comment: The devil signifies evil for most of the Western world, or in some instances the devil simply refers to our character defects. G.G. uses the words "missing the mark," which is the literal translation for the Greek word for "sin" that we use in the Bible today. People see the devil, Satan, Lucifer, and the Angel of Darkness as our lower nature, character defects, and the temptations of the carnal world. For those who were ever involved in satanic cults, these images take on the added dimension of malicious intent and turning from God by choice, not accident.

26. Olya K., age 27, AA, NA, and OA, two years in the program, Russia

Context of the Dream: At nine months I worked my 6th Step, but was very afraid of the changes. If God took all of me and I was entirely ready to have Him remove my defects, what would be left? I would be empty. I got depressed for days because I thought the Step wasn't working. Then I went to a meeting and listened. People were talking about their blessings and love in the program, and I came to realize that when God took my defects, I would have the good stuff left.

Dream: I was in a line of sacrifice to a cosmic being. When we reached the opening or "mouth," we gave all that we had—clothes, money, everything. They swirled around in a circle before entering the opening to be absorbed or digested. As I gave everything, I thought, "How wonderful to give it all."

Interpretation: I knew that I had given everything to God and had worked the Step.

Objective(s):   Trust and rely on God

Principle(s):   Willingness

Step(s): 6

Comment: Cosmic beings very often refer to our guides or other higher realms. It is interesting that the items swirled in a "circle" before flying off. A circle is the universal symbol for God and harbingers "without beginning and without end." The fact that this was a cosmic or alien being would show her unfamiliarity with this new life. The "mouth" let Olya know that she was just beginning to swallow the whole thing. (Note: In the Russian language people "eat" their pills and medicine, thus the added importance of the word "mouth.")

27. Lisa, age 29, AA, NA, and ACOA, three years in the program, Wisconsin

Context of the Dream: Lisa was just into a new relationship with a man also in the program. Her sponsor recently moved away and left her feeling abandoned and vulnerable.

Dream: We were looking for a rabbit to take a picture of. Then I was in a room with toys, old toys. I heard a party and couldn't get to it. I went into a white bedroom with a white canopy bed. (I was wearing what I wore when I spoke about addiction to the children.) On the wall was the picture of the Last Supper (like the one that hangs in my sponsor's house) and I was put into the scene. I was sobbing because I thought I was pregnant. Jesus came to me and one of the apostles threw clover at me. I grabbed Jesus' arm and I *felt* it and I knew all would be okay.

Interpretation: Lisa was being asked to examine (take pictures) of her drug past (rabbit, as in white rabbit). She was missing her past (toys and the party she couldn't get to), but needed to relax about it (white canopy bed) and continue her work with herself in order to grow up (speaking to children). She is being told that she was not alone with her sponsor being gone (same picture on the wall) because Jesus is always with her. Lisa is afraid of her new sober life (pregnancy), but is being reassured of growth and good luck (clover).

Objective(s): Examine self; trust and rely on God

Principle(s): Hope, guidance, love

Step(s): 10 and 11

Comment: After this dream, Lisa wanted to know if she really saw Jesus. I told her to ask her Higher Power for a sign. There was a chance that she was pregnant, although she wasn't distressed about this in real life, only in the dream. Lisa began her period fifteen days early. She took that as a direct sign that she saw Jesus, as in "washed in the blood of the lamb"! Taking a picture of anything means to examine the circumstances you are photographing. When we talk to or teach children, we are communicating with our immature (or innocent) persona. This young woman was also sobbing about her pregnancy or new sober life and expressing her distress over the drastic changes in her life. She gave up her old life as a dependent child for the new life as a responsible adult—that's frightening. When Lisa actually *felt* Jesus' arm, this meant that the divine visitation was real—but Lisa didn't know that and so asked for the "sign." Anytime we get a particularly explicit physical sensation through our dreams, such as a touch, kiss, odor, or sound, this is emphasizing the authentic nature of contact.

28. Shelly, age 45, AA, NA, and ACOA, twenty-four years in the program, Alaska

Context of the Dream: At twenty-one years of sobriety, I was just coming out of a horrible period in my life. I landed in Russia working with alcoholics and addicts, and it was really rough. I worried that my career would die in America if I were across the ocean. I considered it a burden to be doing this work even though I viewed it as God's work.

Dream: I observed a man who had long hair like a hippie or Christ. He was trying to fly a huge kite, but it was a little battered and wouldn't fly. He grabbed the end, putting weight on the tail for balance and it lifted into the air. Then he put his feet in place and his arms into the kite stays and began using it like a glider. He flew so high that I wondered if he might crash, but he didn't. He gained control and flew with the air currents, then was able to land safely.

Interpretation: This man was my higher self who was trying to reach God (fly the kite in the shape of the cross). But just having ideals about God isn't good enough to fly. I had to balance myself (weight on the tail). At the same time, I had to live and become my ideals (man puts himself on the stays and assumes shape of cross with kite). As "Jesus so lived the law that He *became* the law," I have to *become* my ideals. Then I can reach a higher consciousness (fly high) and follow God's will for me (follow the air currents) to be safe (land safely).

Objective(s):   Trust and rely on God

Principle(s):   Awareness of God, balance, guidance

Step(s): 11

Comment: This dream revealed to me that Step 11 is not a simple matter of sending my prayers up to God once a day. I must *live* the program. Conscious contact for me is not sending something out to my Higher Power but becoming that something. Flying in a plane—by ourselves or by some other method—often indicates our high ideals, spiritual life, Christ Consciousness, or—some might even say—astral travel. A ground vehicle usually conveys our life journey on earth, while an air vehicle usually conveys our spiritual journey.

Take Meritorious and Moral Action

(Steps 5, 7, 9, and 10)

29. Cheryl, age 29, AA and CODA, one year in the program, Virginia

Context of the Dream: Cheryl was looking for help in a number of other sources besides the 12-Step programs.

Dream: I saw a beautiful light. There was a pale yellow in the center and it was encircled in white light. Emanating from this was a rainbow of colors (pastel and bright hues). Upon seeing this light, I began to feel extremely good. Next, it was as though my inner child jumped from my being, held her hands open, and the light was being held in her hands. Thereafter, the child gave this light to her new therapist, who would not take it.

Interpretation: Cheryl's (beautiful light) mind (yellow) is now encircled by a spiritual consciousness (circled in white light). Her whole life emanates from her spiritual consciousness (colors). The revelations (inner child) are shared with her therapist, who doesn't recognize the value of her work.

Objective(s): Take meritorious and moral action

Principle(s): Revelation

Step(s): 5

Comment: This dream is not only asking Cheryl to share her inner knowledge (light representing her life), but she is warned that her therapist will not understand her revelations. Although it is suggested in the program that a psychologist is an appropriate person to take our 5th Step with, in this case the dream would be telling Cheryl that her therapist isn't the one to take this Step with. Also, her growth is in her hands, not her therapist's. Since the 12-Step programs stress taking responsibility for ourselves, this dream is suggesting that this therapist may not be compatible with Cheryl's new life.

30. Stan S., age 43, AA, eight years in the program, Utah

Context of the Dream: I had just had a big blowout with my mother and finally got to the point where I couldn't take her feeling sorry for herself. She kept trying to make me take sides between her and my father.

Dream: I was being chased by a gray "Big Foot." Behind us was a dark forest. I finally tripped over a barbed wire fence and the Big Foot caught me. I then became the Big Foot. As I was standing by the fence, I saw some old gray bones—a skull and leg bone. I started to crush them with my feet, and then I woke up.

Interpretation: Stan is running into the light (out of dark forest) being chased by a powerful figure (Big Foot—probably his shortcomings that began in his childhood with his mother) who is trying to put her foot down about what he should do. Stan feels the pain (barbs) and is anxious (wired) about his past defects and his mother's desires pursuing him. He is on the fence about this when he finally becomes his own authority figure (becomes Big Foot) and grows up. Nothing is black or white. The present, the past (bones), himself, and his mother are gray issues for him. The past is exposed to the light, and Stan is able to crush it by "putting his foot down" to his mother and pulverizing the past with exposure.

Objective(s):   Take meritorious and moral action

Principle(s):   Revelation

Step(s): 5

Comment: The way we rid ourselves of the past is to write about and then share it. The "Big Book" says about our past, " ... he pushes these memories far inside himself. He hopes they will never see the light of day. He is under constant fear and tension ... "[3] We are told that these will be "cast out" once we take the 5th Step. And later we are requested to ask God to remove our defects. Getting rid of old bones, shadows, dirt and mud, warts, pusy sores, deformities, cleaning house, etc., usually refer in some manner to our "cleaning-house" Steps from 4 to 10. This dream for Stan is referring to the 5th Step because he is exposing the past to the light, which is what we do in the confession Step. The dream is a double-meaning dream in that it is giving Stan a message about how to deal with his mom, "put your foot down," and how to clear up the past defects, "expose them to the light."

31. G.G., age 64, AA and OA, twenty-four years in the program, California

Context of the Dream: I had this dream after I was on the program for two or three months.

Dream: There was a prolific green vine growing in my room near the window. Light cascaded over everything. There were some large cockroaches crawling around.

Interpretation: This dream was telling me I was growing, but I had some bad stuff in with the growth.

Objective(s):   Take meritorious and moral action

Principle(s): Humility

Step(s): 7

Comment: Sometimes the action a dream is asking us to take is implied. This dream does not directly say, "Get rid of the bugs," but it is implied. We also have to look for the implied instructions in dreams. The implied instructions in this dream or any dreams with worms, bugs, or maggots is to get rid of them as soon as possible! When they crawl around and stink up our dreams, we are being asked to do away with the defects that are "bugging" us or others or infecting our lives. Many dreams come with implied instructions. If something is on fire in a dream, it is understood that we should put it out; if we are unhealthy, it is implied that we need to seek health; if we are speeding, we need to slow down, etc.

32. Robea, age 49, Alanon, fourteen years in the program, Idaho

Context of the Dream: The relationship with the man I lived with after my divorce was becoming a real struggle. I was determined, however, that I would not fail at it.

Dream: Clay and I were in a bathhouse. I was naked, and he and others were not. I squatted down to a brackish puddle on the floor and tried to wash in it, but couldn't manage the task. I then took a nice hot shower in crystal clear water that sprayed far beyond me like a spotlight. A woman came back, and we went to the edge of the cement floor. Below in the dirt was one quarter and hundreds of golden pennies. Some were in red wrappers. I reached down to pick up the pennies and fifty in a wrapper came up one at a time. They were the wheat-stamped pennies.

Interpretation: The relationship between Clay and Robea needed cleansing (bathhouse); however, she was being open about things (naked) and he was hiding something (clothed in bathhouse). She tried to work out the relationship (wash in dirty puddle), but couldn't manage. She was going to see the truth (clear water) and would be cleansed of the old relationship (alone in shower). Robea would be recognized by others (spotlight) when changes (change=coins) occurred in her life. From a very dirty situation (dirt) would come small but valuable changes (wheat pennies).

Objective(s): Take meritorious and moral action

Principles(s):   Humility and honesty

Step(s): 7

Comment: The humility in this dream was illustrated by Robea's nakedness (exposure), while others chose to conceal things. She then got down on the floor and tried to make the best of a difficult situation, which wasn't working. She cleaned herself in the "light" of truth from a crystal clear well of spirituality. She was ready for God to remove her defects. After this, changes would begin in her life, probably without Clay since he wasn't there after her cleansing. This dream did turn out to be one of many prophetic dreams about her destructive relationship with this man that eventually led to his leaving. The important message of this dream was her need to stay cleansed and in the light of God.

33. Cheryl B., age 43, Coda, eight years in the program, Oregon

Context of the Dream: My daughter was shooting drugs, and everything I had done to help didn't. I tried everything and had even started turning her dealers into the cops trying to cut off her supply.

Dream: My daughter died of a drug overdose. I went to her house, and it smelled of vomit and urine. There were clothes on the floor, beer bottles, and dirty dishes, and the place was filthy. She lay dead in her room. I felt she was now at peace. I cleaned her and put on clean clothes. I laid her in a clean bed and shut the door. Then as her druggy friends and dealers came to see her, I would say, "Come in, honey, Lisa's in the shower." They would come in, and I shut the door and shot them in the head, killing them. Then I'd lay them out in the kitchen, one by one. I don't remember feeling anything but relief, that I did what I had to do.

Interpretation: Lisa's addiction is killing her, and her mother is being asked to prepare for this possibility. But the dream is also suggesting that in order for her mother to be "at peace," she would need to stop enabling. Taking care of her daughter, changing her clothes is "death" to Lisa. The dealers and friends are Cheryl's enabling defects (she lies that Lisa is cleaning up in the shower). She is asked to stop the dysfunctional thinking (shoot in the head) about nurturing (kitchen) her daughter. It is what she has to do (kill off defects).

Objective(s):   Take meritorious and moral action

Principle(s):   Humility, justice, discipline

Step(s): 7

Comment: Cheryl says, "Taking care of Lisa in my dream can be seen as my last chance to take care of my daughter or my last act of co-dependency." Cheryl is being asked to get rid of her character defects by changing her thinking. Again, this is implying her need to take Step 7 and ask for her thinking to be straightened out. Shooting something usually means we need to kill off an attitude, thought, characteristic, activity, or relationship. Unfortunately, this dream is also warning that Lisa may, in fact, die of her addiction before anyone can help her.

34. Luanne, age 40, NA, one year in the program, Washington

Context of the Dream: Luanne had finally decided to try the NA way and was keeping close contact with her sponsor. She just received her ninety-day key tag and had this dream.

Dream: I had acquired many different-colored key chains and had them dangling from my purse, hanging on my coat, buttons, and various places on my clothes. When I entered the room, everyone was giving me dirty looks. People started walking up to me and ripping these key tags off and would say, "Branded, branded, branded." The music from the TV series *Branded* was playing in the background.

Interpretation: This dream was telling Luanne that her pride (displaying the key tags) at being sober was causing her problems with others and herself (dirty looks). It is "branding" her as prideful and boastful, and she was likely to lose all if she didn't do something about it.

Objective(s):   Take meritorious and moral action

Principle(s):   Humility

Step(s): 7, 9, and 10

Comment: Often we see that "pride goeth before a fall" with people in sobriety. They get so proud of their accomplishment of not taking that first fix, pill, or drink and forget where sobriety really comes from and what we have to do to stay clean and sober. Working our programs is not just a matter of collecting chips and taking pride in coming to meetings. It is a matter of putting into practice our principles on a daily basis. When we fail to take to heart the true meaning of spirituality, our dreams will be quick to let us know.

35. Shelly, age 45, AA, NA, and ACOA, twenty-four years in the program, Alaska

Context of the Dream: I was working in Russia and the need was so great in all areas of recovery that people often asked me to give lectures or advice about everything! I was an American and so perceived as knowing it all.

Dream: I see multicolored shells—yellow, lavender, brown— so pretty. I give them to the kids. Then I see dolls lining the passage and pass them out. I remember that they're not mine and take them back. I then give out more shells.

Interpretation: I am doing my work by sharing my experience, strength, and hope (multicolored shells and my name is Shelly). I am playing around in other fields (dolls that represent other professionals), but am asked to take back what I have given in other disciplines and stick with what I know (my shells).

Objective(s):   Take meritorious and moral action

Principle(s):   Restitution

Step(s): 9

Comment: We are told on the program that we can't give what we don't have. In this case I was trying to give information on family therapy, prevention, psychotherapy, and other related fields. My expertise is with addiction recovery, and this dream was telling me to cancel plans for doing lectures in areas for which I was not qualified and stick with what I know. Notice how my dream used "shells" as a way to talk about me. Names can be presented as puns to get across a point—such as "Herman" meaning "her man," "Stewart" meaning a "steward" or "guide," "Mary' meaning "merry" or "marry," "Klingon" meaning we are "clinging on" to something, or "Yeltsin" meaning "yelling is a sin." We should try to search for these types of messages contained in names in our dreams and visions.

36. Karma, age 12, Alateen, three months in the program, Idaho

Context of the Dream: My daughter Karma had begun stealing money from my purse and business office. So when the Alateen funds disappeared, I accused her. When I confronted her, she denied everything, blaming other kids. That night she had this dream.

Dream: God came in the front door and told me He would kill my mother if I didn't tell the truth. I refused, and our cat, Beeper, turned into a lion and went into the bedroom and killed Mom.

Interpretation: This was a warning from God that Karma's animal nature (cat) was impure (this cat was black and white—spotted and impure) and would go wildly out of control (turn into lion) because of her lying (lion) and destroy our relationship (kill me).

Objective(s): Take meritorious and moral action

Principle(s): Restitution, discipline, confession

Step(s): 9 and 10

Comment: This nightmare woke her up, and she ran screaming into my room and confessed and begged forgiveness. It was a graphic and terrifying lesson for her. Animals embody our animal nature or take on the characteristics of the animal depicted. The tamed domestic creatures refer to our more human qualities, and the wild animals refer to our more instinctual, base, and uncontrollable traits. Animals that we know, our pets, have additional individual qualities that we come to know as they live with us. When we dream of our pets, we must consider the additional traits that we come to know and love (or hate) in them. Beeper, our cat, had tinnitis, which produced a buzzing sound that anyone could hear emanating from his head. He had a hard time hunting because he couldn't stalk his prey—the buzzing always alerted them. Therefore, this dream was additionally telling Karma that she couldn't very well hide this from me; I had already been alerted to her lying.

Service to Others

(Step 12)

37. Drew, age 44, AA and NA, twelve years in the program, Canada

Context of the Dream: Drew was working with people and beginning to think he had all the answers. He had a disagreement with someone on the program who told him we can only really help ourselves. He asked in meditation if he could really help anyone or not.

Dream: I am in a stadium-like place and all kinds of people are showing off their stuff. Shelly was there. Another guy I was seriously working with veered off and didn't talk to me. Shelly was friendly, then went to a table and ate. I tried to catch her eye and couldn't, so I went down a passage. A man said it would cost me $15 to get in. I paid it and woke up.

Interpretation: The people that Drew was working with were there displaying their needs. Never-the-less, one guy doesn't listen to him, but goes his own way and Shelly nourishes herself. Drew has a narrow path (passage) to a place where he can support these people (under stadium), and it is with love (he gives love—15 = 6 = love).

Objective(s): Be of service to others

Principle(s): Love, selflessness

Step(s): 12

Comment: Sometimes we think that service is convincing others we are right. Drew was beginning to think he knew what was best for others as opposed to sharing what he had learned. This was evident to people around him—but as so often is the case, he couldn't see it. He would get very frustrated that others didn't do things exactly as he thought they should. The fact that he was in a stadium showed that he was having the problem with a lot of people. It also suggests that his behavior is visible to everyone. Since dreams can be on several levels, it simultaneously is telling him that until he gets to the root of the behavior in his subconscious (underneath), his attitudes will cost him the love (he had to pay $15) that he craves.

38. Jeanette, age 31, AA and NA, nine years in the program, Colorado

Context of the Dream: With one year of sobriety to my credit, I had this dream.

Dream: My cousin Susie came to live with me, and I gave her a pink dress to wear and pink shoes to match.

Interpretation: When my cousin comes to live with me, I should give her a foundation of love—pink shoes and dress—nothing else can match that.

Objective(s): Be of service to others

Principle(s): Love

Step(s): 12

Comment: Jeanette explained the outcome, "My aunt called me one year later and begged me to let Susie live with me. She was a screwed-up, nineteen-year-old drug addict and I didn't want to, but I did out of respect for my aunt. I remembered the dream which told me to love Susie. I did just that, and Susie got clean and sober. I never told my cousin that she *had* to get clean; I just loved her like my dream said and it worked." Colors of clothing tell us about the image we give to others (bright red dress could mean a sexy image) or what we should do for ourselves (peach blouse could mean to try relaxing) or how we should protect ourselves (wearing a white wool coat to follow Christ like sheep). To give an article of clothing would be telling us what we are or should be giving to others. When others give things to us, it is an indication of what we are receiving from them. This can be both positive and negative. If someone gives us a black purse, it may mean that the value of the gift is yet unknown to us. If they present us with a red scarf, it may be saying that they are inflaming our attitudes toward something. Clothes reflect our image to others, what they observe, and what we present to the public.

39. Kiley, age 18, AA, four years in the program, Idaho

Context of the Dream: I had this dream a year before it happened to me, and I feel it was warning me of what would be coming so that I could help the woman I was with.

> *Dream:* There was a huge building. It was ornate with propellers and colorful, toylike objects hanging all over it. Later, dreadful things seemed to be happening.

Interpretation: This was literal and precognitive and was warning Kiley not to take the situation as a game for children.

Objective(s): Warning; be of service to others

Principle(s): Usefulness

Step(s): 12

Comment: Kiley shared how this dream helped her to get her and another woman through a formidable ordeal. "A year after this dream, I went with a young Russian woman, a newcomer to the program, to St. Petersburg. I saw this children's store which was just like in my dream, with all these incredible toys and propellers decorating it. I remembered my dream and knew we were in for a rough time. I didn't tell her because I didn't want it to be a self-fulfilling prophecy, but I prepared myself. Soon we found ourselves in a small apartment with a drug addict cooking up drugs in the kitchen, shooting up, and nodding out. We went to St. Petersburg to play, but it was a disaster, and I know the woman would have used [drugs even] if I hadn't been there." After studying our dreams for a while, we will begin to get the pattern of when we are likely to have precognitive dreams. Mine are almost always one month, two months, or one year to the month of when they occur. When I do my dream reviews, I always pay close attention to these time frames to compare to my current situation and see if I need to be concerned about something.

40. Shawn, age 18, Alateen, two years in the program, Wisconsin

Context of the Dream: Shawn was having a rough time because his girlfriend lived with very strict parents and he couldn't see her unless she was in school. They wanted to live together, and Shawn said that he would help her leave her parents.

> *Dream:*   I saw a mermaid and she was unhappy. She wanted to get away and said I was the only one who could help. I took her from the water and looked and looked, but she died before I could find another pool.

Interpretation: Shawn's girlfriend was in a lot of emotional distress (mermaid comes from water). He is told not to get carried away with emotion (carry from the water) and "rescue" her or it will kill their relationship (she dies).

Objective(s):   Be of service to others

Principle(s):   Love

Step(s): 12

Comment: Again, this is showing how sometimes in order to help, we have to leave people alone to do their own work. Shawn cannot do for his girl friend what she has to do for herself. He will kill the relationship if he "carries" her. Shawn did back off, and in several months his girl friend was able to leave on her own and they moved in together. In our program we say, "Carry the message, not the person." The reference to the mermaid was also his fantasy of her. It demonstrated how his ideas of this girl and his ideas of love were more storybooklike than the real world.

41. Shelly, age 45, AA, NA, and ACOA, twenty-five years in the program, Alaska

Context of the Dream: I had gone to an AA meeting with a friend. It was a new meeting area for me, and I didn't like the way the leader was chairing. He asked the group for a topic instead of picking it himself, and everyone was silent for a long time. "Oh, you're all well now?" he asked sarcastically. I copped an attitude about this and persuaded my companion to walk out with me in the middle of the meeting, telling her that old-timers expected more from the meetings than insults from the leader.

> *Dream:*   The Loving Care® in my hair washed right out and my hair was so dull. Gray roots had taken over and I was bothered by this. I wondered if I should change products to bring the shine back to my hair.

Interpretation: My loving thoughts (Loving Care® for the hair) was all washed out. The root of my problem (roots) was old thinking (gray hair) which was dulling my mind. I needed a new attitude (new product) to bring the light back to my thoughts.

Objective(s):   To be of service to others

Principle(s):   Love, usefulness

Step(s): 12

Comment: I was in need of an attitude adjustment in working with others. It was my responsibility as senior member to be an example of "how it works"—some example I was. Besides the clever manner in which my subconscious picked a product name to get directly at my shortcoming, the use of this symbol inferred how I was to correct the shortcoming. "Loving Care" has to be washed into the hair. One former TV ad used the jingle, "Wash that gray right out of your hair," which expresses to me that I need to clean up my old thinking to gain the new thinking and shine.

42. Shelly, age 45, AA, NA, and ACOA, twenty-four years in the program, Alaska

Context of the Dream: When I first began to work in Russia, I had several warning dreams that were unclear to me. In one I gave a seminar and people failed to listen, and in another I wanted to work in a grocery store but someone else took my job. A friend in Moscow used to argue with me because I helped so many people. My name was listed with the general service office and, being an American, many Russians came for help also. It got very demanding at times and I went to bed exhausted many a night. My friend didn't want me working with anyone we didn't know—no strangers, even if they were on the program! She accused me of being a workaholic (or 12-Stepaholic) and that I was practicing sick co-dependent behavior. I wondered if she might be right because I'd had the warning dreams. I asked for clarification.

> *Dream:*   There was an accident, and a person was hurt and needed to go to the hospital. The medics came and put the victim on a stretcher. They asked if I would help by lying on top of him to keep him warm and straight. I said, "Yes, but I must go to the bathroom first." I did go to the bathroom and returned. They laid me over him and bundled us together. I realized I would only go as far as the hospital.

Interpretation: The dream was telling me that indeed I should help when asked to work with addicts to keep them alive (warm) and off drugs (straight). I must make sure to do my cleaning-house Steps 4 through 9 (go to bathroom) so that I am fit to help. However, my job was only to get them to the appropriate program (to the hospital) and others would take over from there.

Objective(s):   **Service**

Principles(s):   Love and duty

Step(s): 12

Comment: One of the popular mission statements in AA is, "When anyone anywhere reaches out for help, I want the hand of AA to be there." At the same time, we must take care of ourselves or how effective can we be? In this dream I was being told that I can do my service best by getting others the help they need and then allowing them to carry on from there. I mustn't try to do all the work myself. "Using the toilet" as a symbol for us in the program almost always refers to the "cleaning-house" Steps. Steps 4 through 9 contain the process of eliminating our past wrongs and character defects and are well illustrated by getting rid of the crap in us!

Relapse Dreams

43. Prudy E., age 42, AA and NA, three years in the program, Washington

Context of the Dream: Being an addict, I never forget the feeling I had after going through the complete procedure of shooting up and the fear involved in doing so. I've had numerous dreams of relapsing into my addiction.

Dream: I was getting high with an i.v. and actually felt myself getting high and woke up with tremendous fear and guilt.

Interpretation: I experienced a lot of fear and pain about using drugs. After waking up and realizing it really was just a dream, I felt rewarded.

Purpose: To reinforce sobriety

Comment: Prudy said of her relapse dreams, "I believe God gives me the reminders I need, and some of these reminders are in the form of dreams. I don't have too many of these types of dreams any more, but it seems they just come along periodically when God sees fit. He doesn't let me forget where I came from." The i.v. in this dream was showing her that once she started, it would be a continuous process (i.v.'s are continuous drips into the vein) and not an on-again, off-again slip.

44. Dad, age 42, NA, one year in the program, Colorado

Context of the Dream: Being in the program for the wrong reason led me to leave the program. I went back out and used drugs, but the message of the program stuck with me. The fellowship said that God loves me, and it exemplifies a God of my understanding and not anybody else's. When I came back to the program and had six months for the second time, I had a dream. By then I had figured out that God gave me emotions for a reason. He expected me to feel them and grow as a result of them. They aren't meant to be buried underneath drugs.

Dream: Somebody offered me a joint and I said, "No." Then somebody else handed me a straw and a line of coke. I said, "NO!" Then I turned around just in time to stop an arm coming at me with a needle. I grabbed it and said, "No, I don't do drugs any more!"

Interpretation: I knew then that I didn't have to do drugs for any reason.

Purpose: To reinforce sobriety

Comment: Research from the Maudsley Hospital in London

shows that about one-third of all people addicted to cigarettes have "I've blown it" dreams. However, two-thirds of people who maintain their abstinence have had them, so it looks as if relapse dreams could be a predictor of long-term success. One theory for this can be that it is a way for the subconscious to rehearse how awful it would be to use them again. This is not to say that we shouldn't look at these dreams as warnings, because sometimes relapse dreams *are* warning us what will happen if we don't take measures to prevent it.

45. G.G., age 65, AA and OA, twenty-five years in the program, California

Context of the Dream: I was 160 pounds at the time, and I wasn't paying attention to my weight. I had reached that amount, which was acceptable to me, in OA. I stopped my meetings because I'd hovered at that weight for years and never thought there would be a problem with it again.

   Dream: I got on the scale and was 180-something headed for 190. I was horrified, not thinking I was that heavy.

Interpretation: Precognitive

   Purpose: Warning

Comment: G.G. remarked on her dream, "I paid absolutely no attention to this dream and slowly gained the pounds just as it warned I would." Everything that ever happens to us is first rehearsed in dreams. This does not mean that everything in a dream scene is going to happen to us! However, as we record and *review* our dreams every few months, we begin to understand which types of dreams are precognitive and which are symbolic. This is the most difficult aspect of dream interpretation and transformation—which dreams are literal, and how do we distinguish one from the other? The only answer for this is diligence and discipline.

46. Billy N., age 28, in detox, Indiana

Context of the Dream: Billy was in detox for the first time after she failed to stay clean and sober by just going to meetings.

   Dream: I was smoking caine (rock) with a man from AA. I was afraid to go back to take a piss test, and I was afraid to go back to AA.

Interpretation: Literal

Purpose: Warning and precognitive

Comment: Billy had this dream just five days before she began her slip. She found herself smoking crack with an ex-boyfriend from AA, just like her dream warned her. Now, when Billy has this type of dream, she will know that it can lead to a slip and she can take measures to prevent it.

47. Tom, age 56, SA and Coda, five years in the program, Tennessee

Context of the Dream: Since I am a minister, it was particularly hard for me to realize I had a problem with sex. I had several dreams where I slipped, and they seemed very real.

Dream: I was with a woman in my parish in a sexual way.

Interpretation: This was a literal warning about what could happen if he were not diligent about his recovery.

Purpose: Warning

Comment: Tom mentioned, "It seemed so real, and I was humiliated because I didn't want to let my wife down. I think these dreams let me know how much it means to me to be true to my wife and my spiritual ideals." Dreams about sex usually refer to our need to merge with higher ideals or the spiritual traits that we admire in others. However, for someone in Sex Anonymous the sex dreams take on an entirely different perspective.

48. A.J., age 38, NA and CA, six months in the program, Virginia

Context of the Dream: I didn't go to one of my CA meetings and was feeling guilty about it.

Dream: I went and bought an eightball of crack and got one of my girl friends to smoke it with me at my home. I was putting big pieces in the pipe and kept on smoking until it was gone. The dream was so real that it woke me out of a dead sleep.

Interpretation: Warning

Purpose: To continue her meetings and other forms of recovery

Comment: A.J. remarked about her dream, "This dream changed the way I was. I am glad that I had that dream because it woke me up to reality. I saw that I couldn't live like that, and I am glad that I go to meetings and therapy and see a counselor." Relapse dreams can make us feel horrible about ourselves. I've talked to hundreds of people who have had them, and they continually mention how *real* they seem. Often people think their dream relapses were real for a few minutes when they awaken, before it dawns on them it was simply a dream. Our subconscious communicates with us and gives us these dreams as a precious gift. "See how you will feel?" our higher self asks. In relapse dream after relapse dream, whether it is a drugging, sexual, smoking, or gambling slip, people tell me how grateful they are to have experienced the slip without really slipping. These are "wake-up" calls in our sleep!

49. Tanya, age 28, AA and NA, one year in the program, Ukraine

Context of the Dream: Tanya had just used narcotics but was lying to her group about it, thinking that just "once" wouldn't hurt anything.

> *Dream:*   I was with my old friend who had died of narcotics. By him was a needle and he offered me drugs and I answered, "No, I will die." He answered, "I died, why don't you want to?" "I'm so young," I replied. He said, "I was also young and I didn't want to die." He wanted to wash the needle in a dirty mud puddle, and I saw a clean well and I wanted to clean it in that well.

Interpretation: This guy represents her addiction talking to her. He wants her to start drugs again, but she is "too young." Her disease answers that he died when young, too. Tanya had joined AA at a young age, twenty-six. Tanya "killed" her addiction when she got clean, and the addiction did not want to die. He washes the needle in dirty water, which is her feeling of being "dirty" with her group about her "slip." She wants to wash it in the clean well and "come clean" about her slip.

> *Purpose:*   To warn Tanya to be honest or she will die with her addiction

Comment: Tanya kept her secret for about six months before she "came clean" with her group. It bothered her very much, and she was lucky that her lingering dishonesty didn't lead directly to another slip and death. For addicts of any kind, disease comes in many forms. Often, as with Tanya, addiction manifests as a person who has died from our disease. The dependency appears as a devil, a joker, a terrorist, a ferocious animal, or even something so graphic as maggots in the brain. Our disease talks to us as though it has a life of its own, and indeed many people feel that it has.

50. Tracy P., age 32, in treatment, Indiana

Context of the Dream: I had this dream six months after I slipped in the program.

> *Dream:*   My husband is driving us over the railroad tracks and we are both drinking. I saw a train in flames and a guy burning on the train. Then the train came back our way and the man was screaming, "Help me, help me." I made eye contact with him and he was black. I begged my husband to go back. I told the burning man to jump, and he did and hit his head and died. Everyone came and acted as if they didn't care.

Interpretation: Tracy and her husband were going to the wrong side of the tracks, and Tracy was not in control of her life (not driving). Her slip to drinking (burning train) was causing her old destructive patterns to return (train comes back). She was crying for help and needed purification (burning). She is told to get sober (jump off the train), and nothing but a complete death of old thoughts (hit the head) will kill the drinking (kills him). Others in her life are tired of it (don't care), and she will have to do this herself.

> *Purpose:*   To show Tracy what her slip is doing to her, her friends, and family and instruct her to get back to the program

Comment: Six months after the dream, Tracy indeed admitted herself to treatment. There were few visitors and few people supporting her, including her husband who offered little assistance. This was just as her dream had warned. People were tired of the problems her drinking caused, and her dream had prepared her for the consequences of her drinking behavior. Her addiction appeared as a burning, dying man with whom she made eye contact. "See me," the disease demands. Remember, making eye contact with someone in our dreams is our subconscious's way of impressing the importance of the message on us. Eye contact is when we look into our own soul.

51. Victor O., age 51, AA, ten years in the program, Poland

Context of the Dream: After I got out of treatment, I planned on meeting my wife for a month-long vacation by car through France, Spain, and Italy. My counselor was appalled as was my group. They kept repeating how I might get drunk on a tour like this after treatment. On the trip, my fear was about the self-fulfilling prophecy. On the first of December, I woke up screaming, trembling, and sweating.

Dream: There was alcohol all over me, vodka pouring on me. I was drinking it, breathing it, absorbing it through my skin. I got drunk and wild. Still in the dream, I was fearful. I woke up, looked around, and felt nauseous and scared.

Interpretation: This was a "what-if" dream, having Victor get in touch with how horrible it would be to drink.

Purpose: To reinforce sobriety

Comment: This is one of the most intriguing dreams I have come across in explaining just how creative our higher self or Higher Power can be in giving us messages through our dreams. Victor woke up terrified. Here is how his story progresses, "My wife looked at me in disbelief. I told her my dream. 'It was just a dream,' she said. 'You are sober; don't worry.' I wouldn't listen. Still trembling I kneeled to pray. It didn't help. I was in a heavy fog of fear, remorse, guilt. Was my group's prophecy to be fulfilled?

"I grabbed *Twenty-Four Hours a Day.*[4] I opened it to December 1 and read, in growing disbelief, the AA thought for the day:

" 'The thoughts that come before having a slip are often largely subconscious. It is a question whether or not our subconscious minds ever become entirely free from alcoholic thoughts as long as we live. For instance, some of us dream about being drunk when we are asleep, even after several years of sobriety in AA. During the period of our drinking days, our subconscious minds have been thoroughly conditioned by our alcoholic way of thinking and it is doubtful if they ever become entirely free of such thoughts during our lifetime. But when our conscious minds are fully conditioned against drinking, we can stay sober and our subconscious minds do not often bother us.'

"I had quite a few drunk dreams since then, but they did not worry me any longer."

Reassurance and Encouragement

52. Gino P., age 27, no program, New York

Context of the Dream: I gave up alcohol and pot for health reasons and was using the art of meditation to fill the void, but struggling with it. I also gave up the standard American diet and felt deprived.

Dream: I felt like a sun radiant in the sky. The feeling of joyful acceptance, along with an ever-flowing loving energy flooded me.

Interpretation: This dream felt more real than my conscious moments. I'd say it was from a superconscious place in us that never fell.

Purpose: Reassurance

Comment: When we embark on a new road, our guides or higher self like to give us a boost and spiritual encouragement by sending us light in our dreams and visions. Most light in dreams is a form of conscious contact. In fact, most of the dreams we have, whether guidance, relapse, reassurance, or others, are a form of the 11th Step. They are dreams of us trying to touch God or God trying to touch us. Conscious-contact dreams, which use light as a form of encouragement and reassurance, can use sunlight, prisms, rainbows, a light at the end of the tunnel, starlight, light shining through a window, lightning, a spotlight, blue-white lights, lights emanating from gems, and even such magical images as fireflies.

53. Jeanette, age 31, AA and NA, nine years in the program, Colorado

Context of the Dream: I had been only eight months clean and sober and was really confused. I was disconnected and wanted to believe that God would restore me and make me whole, but had to see the larger picture.

Dream: I was painting and fixing up three small houses. I hammered nails, painted the houses white, and joined them together with wooden beams so that they would all be connected.

Interpretation: This was telling me that I was now healing and joining my body, mind, and spirit. I was painting them white to purify myself. They represent Steps 1, 2, and 3—one represents the body (it is a physical disease), two represents the mind (came to believe), and three represents the spirit (turned it over to God).

Purpose: Reassurance from guides or higher self

Comment: This dream was not asking Jeanette to work on her program per se, but was reassuring her that the work she was doing was successful. When three objects or people appear in our dreams, it usually means our body, mind, and soul in some capacity. For Christians this means the Trinity; for program people it means "turning it over" by working the first three Steps. Jeanette was working on and building herself up in a holistic manner. Objects that represent joining the body, mind, and soul are anything that appears in threes, such as triplets, an egg (shell, yolk, and the white), the three little pigs, the trimesters of gestation, triangles, *The Three Faces of Eve*, triathlon, tripod, and three-point landing.

54. Dad, age 41, NA, one year in the program, Colorado

Context of the Dream: Several times during my stay in Vietnam, I was deeply affected by the children. Either the sight of so many orphans, amputees, etc., or else being put in situations where I felt the only way out was to kill children. Most of my nightmares about Vietnam revolved around children. When the program first found me, I really got involved, but I used the Steps for Vietnam recovery, feeling I only used drugs to cover up my guilt and shame; therefore, drugs were not my problem. Nineteen years and nineteen days after I left Vietnam, I had a dream.

Dream: We had made a movie in Vietnam and the filming was over. I and other people were standing around behind some ropes that were separating us from the onlookers. There were children and adults. A woman came up to me and handed me her baby, a Vietnamese baby. I was hugging the baby and the baby was hugging me back. There were tears of joy as I kept getting the message that "It's over."

Interpretation: Dad was being asked to examine (film) his past in a new way. Instead of being an onlooker, become a part of the process of healing (on the film crew side of the rope). He is being offered a new lease on life (baby) and told that the past is over. He is forgiving himself (tears of joy) for his actions with the children (hugging the baby and the baby hugging him back).

Purpose: To learn to forgive self and get on with the solution of life

Comment: Dad wrote of this experience, "I felt that it was such a fearful dream with such a strong message that I knew the message was true. I came to see that everything happens the way it's supposed to in God's own way and in God's own time. I had thought that my life was unmanageable because of Vietnam, not the drugs. I was wrong, but it took clearing up Vietnam with this dream before I could see my drug unmanageability. I wrote something at the end of the 1st Step in my NA text and I've never forgotten it since: 'Where I've been will always be a part of me, but I don't have to live there any more.' "

55. Shelly, age 45, AA, NA, and ACOA, twenty-four years in the program, Alaska

Context of the Dream: I had gone through a nasty divorce and threw myself into the fellowship and service work as a method of healing.

Dream: I was a stripper who didn't take her clothes off. Novel idea and people loved it. I was both male and female. Dove under the water and found lots of gold coins with AA imprinted on them. One had LIGHT on it, and then I found a stack of bills.

Interpretation: I was able to put a new, creative slant on my past (stripping was my profession as a drunk) and present it to the public who liked it. This would be referring to the book I would write about the divorce (novel idea), which would help balance me (male and female). Submerging myself in AA (gold coins with AA on them) and Christ Consciousness (gold coin with LIGHT on it) would be of great value to me and support me on the earth plane (stack of bills).

Purpose: To reassure me that all was well and that I would be taken care of both spiritually and materially

Comment: To be on stage is a way of showing us what we are presenting to others and their reaction. "All the world's a stage," and it is here that we get a chance to express ourselves and be heard. We can launch new ideas and projects by "rehearsing" them first in our dreams and test their probable outcome by going on stage with them.

56. Rosa, teen-ager, in treatment[5]

Context of the Dream: Rosa was just about to graduate from drug treatment.

> *Dream:*   I was in an airplane with my friends from treatment. At one point the plane stopped in Nazi Germany. There was a roller coaster nearby. While in Germany, I heard a voice telling me what to do while I was there.

Interpretation (by Connie Sonera, her therapist):   Rosa was flying high without drugs, and the plane represented this ideal. On her trip Rosa was taking her support with her (friends) and what she learned in treatment. Nazi Germany had to do with parental restrictions and how she viewed them. The roller coaster represented the emotional ups and downs she would go through. The voice was her Higher Power telling her what to do.

Purpose: Reassurance and guidance from her Higher Power

Comment: When we dream of other countries, we must look to see how these countries appear to us. Nazi Germany was quite graphic as restrictions in Rosa's life, Japan can be seen as a spiritual alternative to our Christian path, Hawaii as freedom or "fun in the sun," going to Iceland can be viewed as staying in frozen emotion, France can be a wino's paradise or a love nest, and Saudi Arabia could be viewed as oppression of women. Countries, as well as animals, people, places, or things will take on the attributes that we assign to them. Today, it is not politically correct to have stereotypes about other races or other cultures, but the reality is that we do! Our subconscious does not honor "the politically correct" and will continue to talk to us, using stereotypical examples. What we want to avoid in interpreting our symbols is a tendency not to admit our preconceived beliefs in order to conform.

57. Olya K., age 28, AA, NA, and Coda, two years in the program, Russia

Context of the Dream: Olya was having a lot of bad feelings and really concerned that she wasn't working her program right. She talked to her sponsor, did another 4th Step, but still had a lot of emotional turmoil and it really worried her. She was agonizing over her erratic emotions.

Dream: I was in a new apartment and my family was there. Things were flying around the room, and I was really afraid there was a spirit plaguing me. Several bottles broke, but then I saw the ghost of a small boy smiling. He was only being mischievous and there was nothing to worry about.

Interpretation: Olya was now in a new clean and sober body (new apartment) and in a new relationship with her family (family there). Her emotions are erratic (things flying around) and her nerves are shattered (bottles broken). But her circumstances are nothing to worry about (boy smiling) because they're just troublesome, not permanent or serious (a small boy in Russia represents mischievousness and something to laugh at).

Purpose: To reassure Olya that nothing was seriously wrong with her mind and emotions in her new recovery

Comment: Houses where we live almost always represent our somatic bodies—ourselves from our own perspective. Basements usually mean the past, unconscious, or subconscious, while attics and roofs represent our mind and thoughts. We can stumble upon many new rooms attached to a house that we didn't realize were there. This refers to aspects of ourselves we were not aware of formerly and are slowly uncovering. A stopped-up toilet could be referring to constipation, while bedrooms can refer to our sex life or a need to rest. Stairs can mean going to a higher level as well as a need to work our Steps. Olya's new apartment represented her new self. The fact that she met her parents there was depicting her new relationship to them. If she had seen them in their house, the dream would be referring to their old relationship. If she saw her parents in her childhood home, it would be referring to the origin of her current situation.

Humor

58. Tony E., age 27, NA, six-and-a-half years in the program, California

Context of the Dream: I'm not used to living life without some type of crisis, so as the program began working for me, I had some difficulty adjusting.

Dream: Someone I trusted said, "You're okay and have nothing to worry about." I answered, "I know, that's what worries me!" I woke up laughing.

Interpretation: Literal

Purpose: To chide Tony in a light-hearted way about his propensity to worry

Comment: Voices that speak to us in dreams and visions are often literal and direct messages from our guides and Higher Power. We should pay close attention to voices that speak clearly to us in our dreams. However, we should be cautious of voices that speak out loud while we are awake or in a vision. Elsie Sechrist says that such voices can be "a rebel extension of the subconscious attempting to dominate the conscious or a form of automatism."[6] Usually people who know without a doubt that the voices they hear are divine do not have to worry. The vision and sounds are loving, positive, and with a depth of purpose difficult to explain. When a person wonders where the voices came from, the doubt itself is a clear indication that it was not a divine or higher-self communication. Celestial voices never demand, condemn, or bully. They ask, give options, and shower love. The best method to distinguish between the sound of heaven or the sound of schizophrenia is the content and feelings. Any voices that insist people harm or condemn others is not from God or good.

59. Shelly, age 45, AA, NA, and ACOA, twenty-four years in the program, Alaska

Context of the Dream: In my first few years of sobriety, I was a single woman rearing a child and looking for a partner.

Dream: There was a contest in a popular department store to win a date with a man. We ladies were standing around waiting for the name to come out of the hat. Someone pulled the name out and it fluttered to the floor. I bent over to pick it up because I had won. When I picked it up, I accidentally picked up a sales receipt for the store. I looked up and read the name off the sales receipt, "Does anyone here know a Montgomery Ward?" We all laughed.

Interpretation: I was "picking up" the wrong clues for the men I should date.

Purpose: To let me know in a humorous way that I wasn't getting the right idea about the men I was dating

Comment: Humor is an excellent way for our guidance to tell us things we don't want to hear. As in waking life, when it is easier to hear things couched in humor, it is easier in dreams also. Just because a dream is funny doesn't mean it was sent to entertain us. Some of the most serious messages we receive arrive in "funny" dreams. It is another mode that our higher self uses to open up our ability to accept criticism and let go of obsolete defenses.

60. Jewish man, no program, New York

Context of the Dream: This is a humorous encounter a man had with his Higher Power.

Dream: "He was being visited by God, who wore a typical business suit and carried a derby hat. The dreamer escorted God into his house and showed Him around until they happened upon the man's liquor cabinet. Somewhat embarrassed by the full cupboard, the dreamer explained, 'In case of sickness.' God replied, 'You are well prepared!' "[7]

Interpretation: This gentleman was blessed with a genuine visit from the Higher Power—and at the same time received a humorous reprimand about his liquor supply.

Purpose: Humorous and divine reprimand

Comment: The delightful thing about this dream is its message that our Higher Power doesn't have to be the dour, sour Power of our youth. He can be as merry as He is deadly serious—in other words, our communication with Him in our dreams can be splendid in all sorts of ways—not the judgmental, punishing, angry presentations of some, but a joyful, loving, humorous Source for new understanding of the purpose and process of life here on earth.

Death and Rebirth

61. Charlie, teen-ager, in treatment

Context of the Dream: A patient of Connie Sonera's, Charlie had this dream three times in one month.

Dream: "I felt cold and then I died. It took about thirty seconds for the brain to die and my soul to leave my body. During those thirty seconds I felt hot. I saw my blood stop in my body and I grew hotter. I started yelling, 'No! No! Please! God! No!' As I faded away, a bright light hit me and I was warm. It felt good. Then I felt something leave my body. It was my soul. Someone said to me, 'You didn't trust me!' Then I went into a judgment. It was like God and the devil were fighting over who gets my soul. When I did wrong, the devil had my soul. It was hot and got hotter each time I did wrong. Each time I did good, I was with God where it was warm, and God had a white light with a tent of green and very bright. The devil was dark red with a black background. The judgment started when I was a kid, the first time I did wrong and did good. I haven't reached the end yet with the final decision of who got me—God or the devil. Something told me that when I reach a decision that is when I will die."[8]

Interpretation   (by his therapist Connie Sonera): "I told Charlie that this was an important dream since it had recurred three times in the last month. I asked him if his past behavior had bothered him and if he had been worried about heaven and hell. He said yes. Since Charlie had committed acts of vandalism and had been heavily involved in drug use, I felt that this dream was letting him know how his behavior affected him."

Purpose: To show Charlie he had some important choices to make about recovery

Comment: Connie also offered some insight to the death side of the dream. "Because of the topic and the potential of being frightened of it, I offered more guidance on the meaning of the death aspect of the dream. I reassured him that death in the dream was letting him know that when he made the final decision as to his life style, he would have to 'die' to one in order to live the other." Dreams of death seldom literally mean death. We have to die in order to be reborn. Death dreams ordinarily mean that our old self or past is dead and our new life is born. As we said in an earlier dream (#33), when we see someone die or we kill someone, it signifies what is happening to the relationship with that person. Newcomers to the study of dreams are relieved to learn that death dreams don't generally mean they, their family, or friends are going to drop dead. People recovering from addiction have numerous dreams about death and dying, especially as they begin to recover and set off the process of rebirth!

62. Jeanette, age 31, AA and NA, nine years in the program, Colorado

Context of the Dream: I had about one week of being clean and sober when I had this dream.

Dream: I was in the parking lot of the bar and a gang grabs a patron and beats him up bloody. It is so brutal that his skull pops open and his brains spill onto the concrete.

Interpretation: All my old ideas from my drinking days (bar) have to be smashed before I go on.

Purpose: To let her know that tremendous changes have to be made in thinking in order for her to begin her new life

Comment: Death, as stated before, is a transitional state that leads to a new consciousness. In Jeanette's dream the spilling of the brains was prominent. This emphasizes the necessary changes in thinking and attitudes that must be made to give up the old. In the "Big Book" we say, "Some of us have tried to hold on to our old ideas and the result was nil until we let go absolutely." [9] It is the message of *absoluteness* to which dreams about spilling brains, shootings in the head, and total carnage are referring.

63. Claire, age 40, Coda, newcomer, Virginia

Context of the Dream: Claire was having trouble in her marriage and had just revealed the sexual abuse she suffered as a child.

Dream: My husband and I were in a South American revolution in an army jeep. I was carrying a gun. I went to this stone building with no windows and there were dead babies everywhere. One was still alive, and I was going to get it, but my husband said there wasn't time. He pulled me out, and then we took off in the jeep, but I kept thinking I should have gotten that baby.

Interpretation: There was a revolution going on in Claire's life and although she had the power to change (she carried a gun), she allowed her husband to be in control. Claire was hiding (no windows) the traumas (dead babies) of her past. Her husband didn't want her to mess with her past (don't take the baby) even though Claire knew she needed to.

Purpose: To convince Claire to take charge of her own growth which she already had the power to do.

Comment: Claire said of her dream, "To me, the baby who was still alive but being left behind was I. This dream made me start working on myself more." I would also suspect that one of the problems facing this marriage had something to do with drugs, as the "revolution" was taking place in South America where most of the drugs for this country are grown. Dead babies almost always refer to potentials or opportunities we have let slip by or failed to realize.

Precognition and Warnings

64. Lin, age 51, Coda, six years in the program, Virginia

Context of the Dream: This occurred when I going through an unhappy period of my life.

Dream: Yoj-Anon was a demon who was threatening to throw me off a cliff if I didn't wake up.

Interpretation: Yoj is "joy" spelled backward. Lin's failure to really practice the principles of the program was at the source of her depression, which is the opposite of joy or "Yoj." If she didn't wake up to it, she would get a terrible awakening (off the cliff).

Purpose: To help Lin see that working the program would bring joy back into her life

Comment: Many times we go to the meetings, but don't actually work the Steps or apply the principles in our lives. Our dreams will register maximum protest if we have the tools before us, but don't—for whatever reasons—choose to use them. It is interesting to note that the only realistic way to pronounce "Yoj" would be "yo," so that the dream is saying, "Yo, hey you, wake up!"

65. Shelly, age 45, AA, NA, and ACOA, twenty-four years in the program, Alaska

Context of the Dream: I had just been divorced and wondered what all the pain, disgust, devastation, and time out of my life had been for.

Dream: I and a handsome guy went to an open market bazaar and sat on the ground. I saw a building and a door with the word "Head" written above it in blue letters. I made a joke about it maybe being a "head shop." We laughed, but I knew that wasn't what it meant. Then a girl named Susan wrote a review of the story in a magazine. The review continued for pages upon pages, replete with illustrations. It was about a guy and girl who lived in the rural mountains. They were pretty self-sufficient, but one day she fell in a hole and was lost. I looked at one illustration and could see her in the hole with the town close by, but she couldn't see it. I thought I must show this story to my publisher. The story ended with this poem:

> This is like vacationing,
> A little like vacating.
> Meaning in a thousand trees,
> Meaning in as many me's.

Interpretation: Although my life had been bazaar, I was gaining balance (man with me) and getting grounded (sat on ground). I would get ahead by going through the door to Christ ("Head" written in blue letters) who heads my life. The double play on the words "head shop" was referring to my husband who was a drug addict, and being with him had led me away from my spiritual ideals. The review of the girl and guy in the mountains was my marriage; we lived in the mountains of Idaho. I was lost to my world (town I couldn't see), although it was right there. I should write a book about my experience (show to my publisher). The poem was referring to my reasoning abilities and career goals (going on "vacation" or "vacating") during my marriage. The significance of the thousand trees refers to a thousand lifetimes of growth for me.

Purpose: To show me that this was another experience in my spiritual growth and that I should write a book about it to help others grow

Comment: Many times our dreams will help us in our creativity and encourage us to explore areas we hadn't thought of before. I did write the book of this experience, to share my strength with others when they face life's crises. Both the town and the trees were referring to the fellowships of AA and NA. We say in the program that our family is the fellowship. In my marriage, I had forsaken my "family" in AA to please my husband, who hated the program, thus the image of "lost in the hole." The thousand trees suggests my past lives and the thousands of people responsible for my growth in the 12-Step groups.

66. Raymond, age 52, NA, ten years in the program, Utah

Context of the Dream: I was just overcoming a major love affair in my life and was using everything to recover. I used Reiki, Transcendental Meditation, and therapy. I was gaining a lot of insight, it seemed to me.

> *Dream:* I had a Reiki appointment with one of my clients and I pulled the motorized wagon up the steps behind me. I was upset with someone because I had to use those steps to pull the wagon up the hill to my apartment. The steps were very wide, more like landings. They were made of concrete. At first I tried one set of steps, but found that I was on the wrong side of the fence, and I turned around and came back down to the bottom, then went back up the steps on the right side.

Interpretation: Raymond was trying to speed up his recovery (motorized wagon), but was finding it hard to get well (struggle uphill). His guides told him he had to use the 12 Steps because they were clear or "concrete" in nature. It annoyed him, and he tried to do it his own way (on the wrong side), but he relented and worked them the right way (right side).

> *Purpose:* To show Raymond that working the program the way it is intended will help him more than all his other "methods"

Comment: Often we try so many "paths" that we confuse ourselves and become like the saying "Jack of all trades, master of none." It is admirable to seek new information and keep an open mind for growth, but we can overdo anything. Our dreams will help us stay focused if we scatter ourselves too thin. This is not to put forth that Reiki, therapy, and other sources of help are not good for us—they certainly are. But we have no shortcuts, and trying to speed through the growth or grief process by piling on different forms of help can be more than we can absorb at one time.

67. Shawn, age 18, Alateen, two years in the program, Wisconsin

Context of the Dream: Shawn had this dream three times in a few months. His higher self was really trying to get this communication through.

> *Dream:* There was a tree and, if you went through the tree, you went into a time warp. I went through the tree with friends, and we collected pieces from different times to put all together

to save the earth. We put them in a bag and, although they were light, they threw our car off balance. Then a meteor shower hit us. We finally ejected the pieces out of the tree and we thought we lost them. We found them. One piece of the puzzle was the key to our vehicle.

Interpretation: If Shawn goes through his growth process (through the tree), he will find the pieces that will save his world (the earth). He collects them all and, though it appears easy (light), the effort throws him off balance in his life journey (car). The meteor shower presents guidance from God. He gets to all the parts of himself (ejects pieces from tree) and finds the solution (key) to run his life.

Purpose: To show Shawn that although it is sometimes confusing, if he keeps working at growth, he will find his answers

Comment: Shawn's mother was told that Shawn would be institutionalized his whole life because of ADD, epilepsy, and other handicaps. She refused to believe it and raised Shawn according to the principles of the 12-Step program, devoting their lives to honesty, open-mindedness, seeking growth, truth, and service to others. Shawn flourished in his mother's life style and joined Alateen at age fifteen. He truly practices the principles as taught by his mother and the 12-Step program. In addition to graduating from high school (a miracle in itself), he is now working and has a fiancée. He has been following his dreams for years and uses their guidance in his everyday life.

Dream interpretation and the 12-Step program is not for everyone. There are some who will fear that it conflicts with their religious beliefs, some who will consider it not worth their while, some who will find it amusing, like parlor games, but don't apply the lessons learned, and some who will think it's nonsense. But the thoughts of others are not your concern. Remember that *you* are your main concern. And if you have read this far, it's time for you to get to work. Build your glossary, record your dreams, join a dream group, and start communicating with your Higher Power. You now have a way to accelerate your spiritual growth and activate your sacred heritage with God, that conscious contact with your Creator through prayer, meditation, and dreams.

Appendix I

Listing Your 12-Step Principles

The 12 Steps, as Bill Wilson established them (see Appendix III), are clear and universally recognized as the perfect blueprint by which we can recover our lives. However, as chapter 3 discusses, program participants have to establish for themselves what each Step means, both at the beginning and periodically as they gain time in the program. If you have not already done so, this is the perfect time to begin working out what each Step means to you. Review pp. 42-45 and begin listing the principle or principles associated with that Step, as you understand it. This will help give you a broader base for accomplishing the processing of your program dreams.

The principle should be one word or a brief phrase. When we fill in the principle for each Step, it is advisable to read about the Step in our basic program text. This can be one of a number of good choices: *Alcoholics Anonymous; Narcotics Anonymous; Young, Sober, & Free; Overeaters Anonymous; Emotions Anonymous;* etc. However, if your 12-Step program hasn't yet provided you with a basic text, then you can use *Spiritual Secrets of Learning to Love* by Lin Cochran (A.R.E. Press). This is an excellent book that explains the 12-Step principles and how to practice those principles in everyday life.

As you consider options, you might want to discuss them with your sponsor. Know why you believe that a particular principle belongs with the working of the Step you connect it with. Principles are the fundamental truths and the motivating forces upon which our rules of moral conduct are based. The entirety of the 12-Step program is founded on meritorious, moral thoughts and deeds— in other words, PRINCIPLES.

Here is a partial list of the principles that you may want to consider in making your 12-Step list: acknowledgment, admission, conscientiousness, consistency, courage, discretion, divine serviceability, ethicalness, equitableness, faithfulness, generosity, gratefulness, honorableness, honesty, hopefulness, humility, judiciousness, morality, open-mindedness, patience, persistence, perseverance, powerlessness, reasonableness, recompense, reliance on God, responsibility, restitution, revelation, scrupulosity, sincerity, surrender, thoroughness, tolerance, transformation, trustworthiness, willingness. When these principles are coalesced, they can help us turn our lives into ones of integrity, uprightness, and wisdom.

As we gain time and experience, the Step's principles may evolve into different or expanded understandings. Complete the first list now, then do the second list in three to six months. In a year or two, reevaluate what you have done and see if your understanding changes as you gain time on the program. As we do these with the consultation of our sponsors, the help of a basic text on the 12 Steps, and possibly the use of a thesaurus or dictionary, we must ask ourselves, "What is this Step asking me to do?" and "What do I accomplish when I work this Step?" Our answers will help us uncover the underlying principles upon which each Step is based.

	Current Date:	Six Months	One Year Later
1.			
2.			
3.			
4.			
5.			
6.			
7.			
8.			
9.			
10.			
11.			
12.			

Appendix II

Pun Fun in Dreams

As I recall, I was eight or nine when my father first said, "Be careful at the picnic, Shelly, because of all those little uncles running around. I know that it's chilly today, but it'll be hot tamale." I laughed so hard I almost peed in my pants. I like to think that my finding this idiotic pun so hilarious was not so much an indictment of my mental abilities as that of my father's. Unfortunately, my mirth encouraged him, so that when I pouted about having to watch a war movie during Daddy's visitation (he and my mother were divorced), instead of the far more interesting topic of dragons, he assured me it *was* about dragons, "Why, honey, they're *dragin'* a cannon all over the country!" I thought he was the cleverest man in the whole world.

Thus the wonderful world of word play opened up to me. My father's simple-minded sense of humor did not grow up along with me, and when, as a young adult, he told me things like, "Don't go out in the woods this fall, hon, it's when the squirrels gather nuts," I wondered if the pun-ishment would ever end.

Apparently not. This planet is peopled with those who find puns to be the seasoning on the entrée of life. Good examples of these areas are my dentist Bob who calls himself "Oral Roberts," a couple I know who met in Transcendental Meditation by "chants," our reverend who boasts of phoning the other parishes "parson to parson," or my new age friends who sport bumper stickers saying, "My karma ran over your dogma." Worst of all is when we're having a perfectly normal *adult* conversation about Mohammed, Buddha, and the Maoist and Taoist philosophies, and some blockhead has to butt in, "I think there's a bit of Confucius about all this!" The person is usually my date!

I gave up completely when I heard a recovery guru charismatically scream on stage, "I am a human *doing,* not a human being!" and the audience applauded as if some Solomonic wisdom had just been bestowed on them. This guy charged $300 a seat to convince everyone to blame everything on their parents and holler goofy little sayings like that! "It doesn't make sense to me, but it certainly made cents for him!" I thought. Well, maybe the guru had a point. After all, it *is* my dad's fault that I hate the Three Stooges and Steve Martin films, but on the other hand I am a writer.

Once I got sober, I thought I would find a higher form of comedy consciousness in the fellowship. But the fun-in-the-pun mentality "rains" supreme on the walls of the clubs, "Know God, Know Peace: No God, No Peace." Okay, I'll admit that is clever—but when learned professionals start saying, "Denial is not a river in Egypt" and "A hangover is the wrath of grapes," I can hear my dad chuckling at me. I have heard in meetings such puns as, "I'm powerless over alcohol and my wife is unmanageable," "I turned my bills and my wife over to the care of God," and "He will restore us to vanity."

It was when I learned that our subconscious uses the pun as a normal part of conversation that I went ballistic. My conscious mind is a rational adult, but my subconscious is like my dad? Yikes! One aspect of our subconscious seems to be a creative Jokester that, since the days of Freud, has delighted in finding ridiculous uses of words and plopping them into the pool of the collective unconscious so that we can "think" or swim. Our subconscious uses words that rhyme, words that sound alike but mean different things, words that can be taken apart to form other phrases, and any crazy hodgepodge of expressions that will deliver a message in a semblance (whether feasible or far reaching) of reality. Following are a number of word-play categories. These are examples of how the subconscious might decide to befuddle our waking conscious mind in the wonderful world of dreams.

Name Homographs: These are names that have a meaning in addition to the person named. On this first list are names which can contain covert messages that our subconscious might ascribe to the figures in our dreams. For instance, Jane, who is dating a guy who is abusing her, has a dream wherein she calls him "Peter" as she opens the door. The dream is telling her that it's time for him to "peter out" of her life. Another woman dreams of having a baby after five o'clock and she names her Joy. This is telling her that after she labors through the 5th Step, a whole new life will be born to her and it will be very "joyful." A man's new supervisor is named Buck in his dream. Buck looms before him at the entrance to the boss's office. The dream is telling him not to "buck" the system at work.

Following is a list of name homographs that can help you recognize hidden messages and double meanings:

Angel, April, Art, Bill, Bob, Buck, Carol, Charity, Christian, Chuck, Clay, Cliff, Crystal, Daffy, Daisy, Dawn, Dick, Don, Dot, Duke, Earl, Eve, Faith, Fawn, Fern, Flint, Ford, Frank, Gay, Gill, Glen, Grace, Grant, Harmony, Holly, Honey, Hope, Iris, Jack, Jade, John, Joy, June, Major, Mark, Mat, Max, May, Mike, Miles, Miller, Miner, Moore, Nick, Olive, Page, Pat, Patsy, Pearl, Peck, Peter, Pierce, Pilar, Price, Rainer, Ray, Read, Reed, Rich, Rob, Robin, Rock, Rocky, Rod, Rose, Rush, Rusty, Rye, Sandy, Sergeant, Shawl, Stern, Stew, Stewart, Sue, Tailor, Trump, Van, Victor, Wade, Warden, West, Will

Word Homographs: These are everyday words in the English language that have two or more meanings. Unless we hear them in a sentence, we won't know to what they are referring. For instance, in a dream someone receives a phone call from an old friend whom he or she ripped off in their drinking days. A servant hands the phone to the dreamer, saying, "It's collect and you should accept." This dream is telling him or her that that person would like to "collect" the debt, and the guide (servant) is telling the dreamer it is time to make amends. A second example is when we see ourselves arguing in a dream with a cop. Our friend tells us, "You're not too bright." This could be our subconscious telling us that we are "dull-minded" for not listening to authorities in our new life—that we are "copping" an attitude and that we don't "shine" with the light of our Higher Power. Both "cop" and "bright" are used in a double entendre expression.

Following is only a partial list of the many homograhic words that our subconscious might use, and we should always see if a word contains another meaning in order to shed more light on what our sleeping reality is telling us:

arm, ax, bark, batter, bear, bill, bitch, branch, bridge, bright, buck, buff, can, case, cast, change, charge, check, coat, coke, conductor, cop, cover, cross, dart, diamond, dirt, down, draw, duck, dump, fall, fan, fast, feel, fine, finish, fire, fired, fly, foot, fork, ground, head, hide, jerk, kind, lap, laps, left, lie, light, like, line, lord, man, mean, note, novel, nut, over, palm, patent, period, point, pot, power, racket, range, rear, relish, right, ring, road, rule, saw, scales, seal, sentence, sharp, short stop, skin, smart, sound, spectacle, spotted, star, step, straight, strong, stumps, suit, tax, top, train, trunk, type, vessel, watch

Homonyms: These are words that sound alike but may be spelled differently. Homonyms include names of people, places, and things as well as words in everyday language. An example of this type is a dream in which a young man kneads dough in his dream. His helper takes the dough and says, "It will not rise in the pot, but only out of the pan in the sun." The interpretation should let him know that even though he "needs" money (dough), it will not "pan out" from growing "pot," but only by trusting in the "rays" (raise) from his Higher Power (sun = Son). A new member to the program could dream about not being able to stand up straight, and a doctor looks at her foot and says, "In order to stand straight on your sole, you must correct the heel." This could mean that the married man she is having the affair with is a "heel" who won't allow her to "heal" and stand straight (upright), causing pain in her "soul." If we think about it, we can probably add twice as many to the list of homonyms that follows:

ant (aunt), bear (bare), bee (B), board (bored), bore (boar), buy (bye), carrot (karat), cellar (seller), cents (sense, scents), chance (chants), cheep (cheap), cheetah (cheater), coughin' (coffin), days (daze), deer (dear), desserter (deserter), Don (dawn), dyeing (dying), eight (ate), eyes (I's, ayes), Finnish (finish), flea (flee), flew (flu), Flo (flow), foul (fowl), Gail (gale), gate (gait), gorilla (guerilla), grease (Greece), hare (hair), Harold (herald), Harry (hairy), heel (heal), herd (heard), hey (hay), higher (hire), hoarse (horse), hoes (hose), hole (whole), Jean (gene), knit (nit), know (no), lion (lying, line), lock (Loch), maid (made), male (mail), Manuel (manual), Mary (merry, marry), meet (meat), miner (minor), Moore (more), naval (navel), need (knead), Nichole (nickel), night (knight), none (nun), not (knot), one (won), or (oar), pail (pale), pain (pane), peace (piece), pier (peer), plain (plane), prey (pray), principle (principal), Pryor (pyre, prior), purpose (porpoise), rain (reign), raise (raze, rays), right (rite, write), roam (Rome), roll (role), Rune (ruin), Russian (rushin'), sale (sail), sea (see, C), seem (seam), sole (soul), son (sun), stare (stair), Starr (star), steak (stake), steel (steal), Sue (Sioux), sunny (sonny), tacks (tax), tail (tale), tailor (Taylor), to (two, too), tow (toe), turn (tern), urn (earn), vein (vane), waist (waste), walk (wok), wanting (wanton), war (wore), wear (where), Webb (web), week (weak), weighs (ways), Wendy (windy), whale (wail), which (witch), whine (wine), Wolfe (wolf), wrap (rap)

Puns with Names: Many names lend themselves to adulteration and can be fashioned to give us sound-alike messages from our sleep. A very religious person might see Saint Thomas wagging his finger at them. The dream is a chastisement to go "to mass." Another person could have a dream wherein the new "baby" on the program is laughing at him or her. In the dream you say, "Robin, go away," even though the name is not really Robin. This sponsor is being warned that the new baby is a thief and will "rob 'em" of energy, time, and valuables and is basically just using others.

On the lighter side there are always the names that people swear are real, like Rusty Pipes, Jason Rainbows, Helen Highwater, Warren Peace, Rock Starr, Jerry Rigg, Hans R. Dirty, Lettice Finder, Bertha D. Blues, Tyrone Shoelaces, and Dusty Rhodes. Our subconscious probably won't be quite so whimsical, but we need to stay alert to the possibility. Take every name in a dream and figure out its double meaning to divulge more layers of metaphors. Here are some of the many possibilities:

Aaron (air on), Abigal (a big girl), Aida (aid a), Alden (all done), Aldrich (all rich), Amazon (amazing), Amos (aim us), Andrew (and drew), Armand (our man), Ashburn (ass burn), Balkan (balking), Bennet (bend it), Bertha (birth of), Bobbet (bob it), Borden (bored 'em), Campbell (camp bell), Coleman (coal man), Conroy (con Roy), Conway (con way), Darrell (dare all), Darren (dare him), Diane (die and), Eleazer (he lies to her), Ellis (hell is), Ellsworth (hell's worth), Everett (ever it), Fillmore (fill more), Fonda (fond of), Freda (afraid of), Gino (gee no), Griffin (grief in), Gunner (gun her), Harmony (harm her knee), Harriet (hurry it, hairy it), Herman (her man), Hunter (hunt her), Isaac (eye sick), Isadore (is a bore), Jasmin (jazz men), Jason (chase 'em), Kendel (Ken doll), Kissinger (kissing her), Klingon (cling on), Laura (lore of), Lemmie (let me), Marian (marry 'em), Melanie (Mel and me), Meredith (Mary's death), Michael (my call), Mikey (my key), Morgan (more gone), Nixon (nix on), Osgood (us good), Philip (fill up), Prescott (press Scott), Raffaello (rough fellow), Reagan (ray gone), Rearden (rear den), Redford (red Ford), Redman (red man), Roberto (rub her toe), Robin (rob 'em), Robinson (rob her son), Roosevelt (rose he felt), Roxanne (Rocks on), Sharon (share on), Sherwin (sure win), Shirley (sure Lee), Skipton (skip town), Soviet (so be it), Stephan (Step on), Swanson (swan song), Sweden (sweet on), Taylor (tail her), Theresa (tear ass of), Thomas (to mass), Toby (to be), Truman (true man), Walker (walk her), Wallace (wall us), Warren (war on), Welborne (well born), Willa (will of), Willie (will he), Worral (wore all), Yeltsin (yellin' is sin), Yukon (you con)

Word puns: These are the same as the name puns and so prolific that it is only possible to give a tiny glimpse of the variations we can come up with. But this will give an idea of how clever our "pun-conscious" can be. In a dream one might see a sponsor stick his or her fingers into the plug receptacle and marvel that it didn't hurt. The dream might be alluding to a need for the sponsor to "socket" to the dreamer. Another person may see a man in a tuxedo serve him or her a tray full of vice-grips. The dreamer may remark, "Sir, I can't eat that!" This would be telling the dreamer that "Sir Vice," with defects still gripping your personality, isn't nourishing to anyone.

This person may be trying to work the 12th Step and forgetting the others which are our foundation. Here are some puns to help get you started:

Alaska (I'll ask her), alligator (I'll get her), arrange (a range), cargo (car go), cauliflower (call her flower), cauterize (caught her eyes), cheetah (cheat her), Chinese (shyness), Christmas (Christ mass), contest (con test), empress (impress), gangrene (gang green), Garden of Eden (garden of eatin'), goodness (God nest), higher self (hire self), incense (in sense), inner space (in her space), ketchup (catch up), kindergarten (kinder garden), knot holes (not holes), lettuce (let us), lilac (lie like), liquor (lick her), managed (man aged), millionaire (million airs), moron (more on), muffler (muffle her), naughty (not he), nirvana (near Vana), orgasm (or gas 'em), paradise (pair of dice), parents (pair ants), people (peep hole), poker (poke her), policeman (pole ice man), psychopath (cycle path), pyramid (peer amid), sausage (saw sage), service (sir vice), smartest (smart ass), socket (sock it), spirit (spear it), sticker (stick her), sun's rays (son's raise), swatter (swat her), tacks collector (tax collector), telephone (tell a phone), tequila (to kill ya), toupee (to pay), tulips (two lips), weekdays (weak daze), which doctor (witch doctor), women (woe men), yoga (you go)

Lexigrams: A lexigram is a way to delve deeply into the subconscious and unlock the riddles of the names of people, places, or things. In a lexigram we find all the sub-words contained in a name by using the letters found in that name. Then we make short phrases or sentences from the words formed, giving us the message(s) contained in the name. For instance, in her book *Star Signs* Linda Goodman's first example is "messiah." She finds all these words contained in that one word:

HE IS HIM . . . HE IS SAME AS HIM . . . HE IS SHE . . . SHE IS HIM . . . HE IS SAME AS ME . . . I AM SAME AS HIM . . . SHE IS SAME AS HIM . . .

This lexigram is as logical and clear as any message could be to those who use their intelligence and intuition.[1]

It seems that the "message" in the word "messiah" is one of unity with the self and the universe.

Lexigraming is not an exercise for beginning dream processors but is for the more advanced. It's not that it is so difficult, but rather that in the beginning we have so many areas to explore that lexigraming is just too multifarious. As dream interpretation and transformation becomes second nature to us, we can turn our attentions to the more in-depth study of lexigraming the names presented in our dreams. The amount of information can be intimidating, so we have to be prepared for more information than we thought we wanted! Here is one dream that I had four years ago that lent itself to lexigraming very well:

I am with Elvis Presley, who is troubled and asking for my help. I tell him he can't be helped in four or five lifetimes without the Christ Spirit. But the Christ Spirit is a gift and, if he receives it, he can be well tomorrow. We were looking in a book together and tears of compassion came to my eyes.

This is a message about my work with chemically dependent people and the books I write to help them. It is also pregnant with symbology in the lexigraming of the name "Elvis Presley," who represents the addicts of the world. His name lexigrams to these words:

Severe pill spree spells sleep; evil eye sees Elvis; Elvis is VIP; sever evil eye; Elvis rises, yes.

In this dream Elvis represents all of us addicts seeking redemption. Although one may be rich in worldly treasures (fame, money, adulation), it all comes to naught before the powerlessness to addiction. In his name we find hidden the words "evil, lies, viper, pyre, vile, spy, leer, piss, servile," and more. We also find that he can rise— "Elvis rises" and "Elvis lives" or "ye rise" and "ye live." We can also consider that he lived in "Graceland." In the dream he seeks my help, and I explain that even in four or five lives he would have a hard time straightening out all the damage he did in this one.

This is true for all of us. With the Christ Spirit (Christ Consciousness, Light, Higher Power, or whatever suits you), it can all be erased and one can be well tomorrow. In the Bible it says, "For by grace are ye saved through faith; and that not of yourselves: it is the gift of God . . . " (Ephesians 2:8) Basically Elvis, being known around the world, represents "addicted" people around the world. I am told to help them by showing them the Christ Consciousness. The reference to reincarnation is telling me not to withhold my metaphysical knowledge (something professionals have warned me not to disclose or I would impugn my credibility in professional circles). Looking in the book represents how to help—write! And the tears signify cleansing and empathy for all the addicts of the world.

This is the second book I have written that combines recovery issues with metaphysical ideas. I believe this work is very important, and it was with the encouragement of my dreams that I am able to traverse this far. I certainly hope and pray for all my readers that they successfully combine their spiritual growth with the interpretation of their dreams and that their sleeping reality is as prolific and productive as mine has been. God bless you and keep you until we meet, as we trudge this road of happy destiny.

Appendix III

The 12 Steps
of Alcoholics Anonymous

1. We admitted we were powerless over alcohol—that our lives had become unmanageable. 2. Came to believe that a Power greater than ourselves could restore us to sanity. 3. Made a decision to turn our will and our lives over to the care of God, *as we understood Him.* 4. Made a searching and fearless moral inventory of ourselves. 5. Admitted to God, to ourselves, and to another human being the exact nature of our wrongs. 6. Were entirely ready to have God remove all these defects of character. 7. Humbly asked Him to remove our shortcomings. 8. Made a list of all persons we had harmed, and became willing to make amends to them all. 9. Made direct amends to such people wherever possible, except when to do so would injure them or others. 10. Continued to take personal inventory and when we were wrong promptly admitted it. 11. Sought through prayer and meditation to improve our conscious contact with God, *as we understood Him*, praying only for knowledge of His will for us and the power to carry that out. 12. Having had a spiritual awakening as the result of these Steps, we tried to carry this message to alcoholics, and to practice these principles in all our affairs.

Appendix IV

The 12 Traditions
of Alcoholics Anonymous

1. Our common welfare should come first; personal recovery depends upon AA unity. 2. For our group purpose, there is but one ultimate authority—a loving God as He may express Himself in our group conscience. Our leaders are but trusted servants; they do not govern. 3. The only requirement for AA membership is a desire to stop drinking. 4. Each group should be autonomous except in matters affecting other groups or AA as a whole. 5. Each group has but one primary purpose: to carry its message to the alcoholic who still suffers. 6. An AA group ought never endorse, finance, or lend the AA name to any related facility or outside enterprise, lest problems of money, property, and prestige divert us from our primary purpose. 7. Every AA group ought to be fully self-supporting, declining outside contributions. 8. Alcoholics Anonymous should remain forever nonprofessional, but our service centers may employ special workers. 9. AA, as such, ought never be organized; but we may create service boards or committees directly responsible to those they serve. 10. Alcoholics Anonymous has no opinion on outside issues; hence the AA name ought never be drawn into public controversy. 11. Our public relations policy is based on attraction rather than promotion; we need always maintain personal anonymity at the level of press, radio, and films. 12. Anonymity is the spiritual foundation of all our traditions, ever reminding us to place principles before personalities.

Endnotes

Preface

1. *12 Steps Illustrated,* Karen Greene (pages unnumbered).
2. *Ibid.*
3. Edgar Cayce reading 5264-1.

Chapter One

1. "Stepping over the Threshold," Marion Woodman, *Noetic Sciences Review,* Winter 1993, p. 10.
2. *Ibid.,* pp. 11-12.
3. Edgar Cayce reading 3175-1.
4. *Dreams and Spiritual Growth,* Louis M. Savary, Patricia H. Berne, and Strephon Kaplan Williams, pp. 54-55.
5. Edgar Cayce reading 5754-1.
6. *Alcoholics Anonymous,* Bill Wilson, p. 25.
7. *The Dream Book,* Betty Bethards, p. 21.
8. *The Edgar Cayce Encyclopedia of Healing,* Reba Ann Karp, p. 25.
9. *Alcoholics Anonymous, op. cit.,* p. 64.
10. "Stepping over the Threshold," *op. cit.,* p. 14.
11. "Dark Side of the Unknown," Patrick Huyghe, *Omni,* September 1993, p. 42.

Chapter Two

1. Edgar Cayce reading 136-7.
2. *Dreams and Spiritual Growth, op. cit.,* p. 57.
3. "Interpret Your Life As a Dream," Daniel Rosen, *Body Mind Spirit,* March/April 1994, p. 67.
4. Edgar Cayce readings 262-130, 436-3, 900-217, 4905-56, and others.
5. *The Dream Book, op. cit.,* p. 34.
6. *Dreams and Spiritual Growth, op. cit.,* p. 30.
7. *The Dream Book, op. cit.,* p. 33.

Chapter Three

1. Edgar Cayce reading 3188-1.
2. *Alcoholics Anonymous, op. cit.,* p. 116.
3. "The Spiritual Dimension of Dreams," Gayle Delaney, *Venture*

Inward, January/February 1992, p. 37.
4. Edgar Cayce reading 900-429.
5. Edgar Cayce reading 3175-1.
6. *Alcoholics Anonymous, op. cit.,* p. 85.
7. Edgar Cayce reading 5754-2.
8. *Alcoholics Anonymous, op. cit.,* pp. 59-60.
9. *Ibid.,* p. 83.

Chapter Four
1. "On Defining Spirit," Rachael Naomi Remen, *Noetic Sciences Review,* Fall 1993, p. 40.
2. *A Little Course in Dreams,* Robert Bosnak, p. 33.
3. Edgar Cayce reading 3976-27.
4. *Ibid.*

Part II
1. *Dreams: Your Magic Mirror,* Elsie Sechrist, p. 241.

Dreams from the Fellowshlp
1. Edgar Cayce reading 3433-1.
2. *Dreams: Your Magic Mirror, op. cit.,* p. 86.
3. *Alcoholics Anonymous, op. cit.,* p. 73.
4. *Twenty-Four Hours a Day* (New York: Walker, 1989).
5. "Dreams Work for Drug Addicts," Connie Sonera, *Venture Inward,* September/October 1990, p. 37.
6. *Dreams: Your Magic Mirror, op. cit.,* p. 33.
7. "Dream Insights: Walking Up to Who We Are," Nancy Pohle, *Reflections,* October 1992, p. 2.
8. "Dreams Work for Drug Addicts," *op. cit.,* pp. 36-37.
9. *Alcoholics Anonymous, op. cit.,* p. 58.

Appendix II
1. *Linda Goodman's Star Signs,* Linda Goodman, p. 427.

Bibliography

Books

Alcoholics Anonymous (New York: Alcoholics Anonymous World Services, Inc., 1939)

This is the basic text of the program of Alcoholics Anonymous and from which all the other 12-Step programs sprang. Many of the groups that haven't written their own basic text use this book in their meetings and to study the Steps. It is known as the "Big Book" and concentrates its message on practicing the principles of the 12 Steps in daily living. Written in 1939, it was terribly courageous at the time. Bill Wilson, the main author and founder of AA, used many spiritual terms (metaphysical, if you will) because he didn't adhere to the strict traditional views of dogma for recovery from alcoholism. It was a spiritual experience that brought him to recovery, and Bill openly shared that with everyone. He insisted that a belief in anyone else's idea of God was not necessary for recovery and referred to God as "Father of Light," "Principle," "Infinite Power," "Universal Mind," "Spirit of Nature," and our "Friend." For those interested in the roots of this amazing program, I recommend reading the chapters "Bill's Story," "We Agnostics," "How It Works," "Into Action," and "A Vision for You."

Bethards, Betty. *The Dream Book: Symbols for Self-Understanding* (Petoloma, California: The Inner Light Foundation, 1983)

This is a rather standard no-nonsense dream book/dictionary. Betty lists the universal meanings of many symbols that those dedicated to dream interpretation have generally come to agree on. I like her straightforward approach to presenting the material. It is from Betty that I picked up the phraseology "three free tools" when referring to prayer, meditation, and dreams. I also particularly like her section "Anatomy of a Dream," which I incorporated in my system of interpretation and transformation. She is a talented psychic, mystic, and spiritual healer, and I recommend her work to anyone.

Bosnak, Robert. *A Little Course in Dreams* (Boston: Shambhala Publications, Inc., 1988)

Robert is so Freudian and psychoanalytical about dream interpretations that for purposes of philosophy or symbol interpreta-

205

tion I wouldn't recommend him. He gets into the anal-retentive, penis-envy analysis that can cast a pall over every natural thought and action possible to humankind. However, on the bright side, he demonstrates some excellent dream exercises that will turn the interpreter into a "creative listener" and makes use of free association and the imagination that are quite befitting any dreamwork group. It's an excellent task-oriented book.

Boushahla, Jo Jean, and Virginia Reidel-Geubtner. *The Dream Dictionary* (New York: The Pilgrim Press, 1983)
These two women give a wonderful overview of what dreams are and how important they can be in everyday living. I particularly like the reliance on the Edgar Cayce material and the fact that they put this dictionary together in their group work over the course of many years. It is very informative on symbology and not only has an alphabetical listing, but a subject grouping as well. They included a helpful chart and explanation on the spiritual centers, endocrine system, and chakras that easily blends the Western and Eastern philosophies for utilization with dreamwork.

Caprio, Betsy, and Thomas Hedberg. *At a Dream Workshop* (Ramsey, New York: Paulist Press, 1987)
This is a wonderful book for the dreamwork groups. It walks people through the process of a dream workshop. The authors use a biblical Christian approach to dreamwork and present dreams as a clear way to reach God and self-actualization. It is from this material that I based the 12-Step dream invocation exercise.

Carson, David, and Jamie Sams. Medicine Cards (Santa Fe, New Mexico: Bear and Company, 1988)
This is not a book, but is known in American Indian circles as the "Animal Medicine Cards." A little like the tarot cards, they can give one a reading about an animal's healing powers, a person's totem, or general information concerning the inquirer. For purposes of dream processing, these are a delightful source of the symbolic interpretation for forty-four animals. These cards will tell you about the animal's characteristics, what it generally means in the Indian sense, and how to apply that to dream interpretation. You'll find these very helpful!

Chetwynd, Tom. *How to Interpret Your Own Dreams in One Minute or Less* (New York: Bell Publishing Company, 1980)

The "one minute or less" part is nonsense, but the author does give a quick, don't-beat-your-head-against-the-wall system for getting at the heart of a dream. We agree on the fact that there is nothing so all-fired mysterious about dream interpretation and that a belief in our own ability to work with dreams is the greatest tool available. Tom, like many others, places too much emphasis on the Freudian approach, but his dictionary is an adequate supplement to other dream dictionaries.

Cochran, Lin. *Spiritual Secrets of Learning to Love* (Virginia Beach, Va.: A.R.E. Press, 1994)

This is a marvelous exploration into the application of the 12 Steps in everyday life. Lin has a very down-home approach to explaining things to her readers and uses her personal experiences so that all will easily identify with her. She has blended the *Search for God* texts with the 12-Step approach to living and has produced a truly fresh look at how we live the 12-Step programs.

Dreams and Dreaming, Library Series on the Edgar Cayce Readings, Vols. 4 and 5 (Virginia Beach, Va.: A.R.E. Press, 1976)

These are a collection of documented case histories on dreams that Edgar Cayce interpreted from his altered state of consciousness. It is recommend that people going into advanced studies of dreams get these volumes and study them closely. They are arduous reading, but worth the time if one wants deep, although obscure, nuances on dream symbology and insights into dreaming.

Goodman, Linda. *Linda Goodman's Star Signs* (New York: St. Martin's Press, 1987)

For anyone really serious about interpreting dreams, visions, and life events this is a must. It is for the advanced interpreter and transformer. Linda discusses thoroughly the numerical significance in our lives, the musical influences, the alphabetical influences, and the astrological influences. It is the most complete book on the culmination of symbolic interpretative influences on our existence that I have ever run across. I find myself constantly using the material presented in her book for my work. The material for the lexigrams and some general philosophy came from her leadership. Linda is not afraid to hang from a limb and share her varied experiences. It is guaranteed that you will learn something new and challenging from her work in the metaphysical.

Greene, Karen. *12 Steps Illustrated* (New York: New Hope Press Book, 1988)

A lovely book that presents the 12 Steps in an ethereal, mystical, pictorial form. The introduction is a comprehensive overview of the beginning of the 12-Step movement. A great gift item.

Holy Bible (New York: The World Publishing Company, undated)

The Bible is a masterpiece of parables and analogies. The concordance is wonderful as an index of symbols, and I highly recommend that Christians use it when they begin making their own dream glossaries.

Karp, Reba Ann. *Edgar Cayce Encyclopedia of Healing* (New York: Warner Books, Inc., 1986)

Although now out of print, this is an excellent reference for Cayce's philosophy and readings on healing from addiction. It not only discusses the physical aspects of treatment, but our spiritual motives and intents. Includes a vast array of physical ailments.

Marshall, Shelly. *The Book of Karma* (Littleton, Colorado: Phantasma Publishing, 1994)

This is autobiographical and is a sharing of my experience, strength, and hope. At nineteen years clean and sober, I had a tremendous tragedy that brought me to my knees. This is my story and how I used the program, dream interpretation, and the Bible to carry me through. It is a practical look at living the program through dream interpretation when it really counts—every day.

Marshall, Shelly. *Young, Sober, & Free* (Center City, Minn.: Hazelden, 1978)

This is an explanation of working the 12 Steps for people under the age of thirty. Whereas the "Big Book" and the *Twelve Steps and Twelve Traditions* are geared toward those over forty, married, and from middle-class America, *Young, Sober, & Free* explores these same principles from the younger, usually single individual who has a with-it outlook on life. This is a more inclusive book for the youngish person seeking growth through the 12-Step methods and has the added advantage of sharing the direct experiences of the young person in recovery.

Savary, Louis M., Patricia H. Berne, and Strephon Kaplan Williams. *Dreams and Spiritual Growth: A Judeo-Christian Way of Dreamwork* (New York: Paulist Press, 1984)

This book makes the most wonderful case for firmly planting the basis of dreamwork in an historical, traditional, and practical quest for God. The authors explain how religious authorities mistakenly came to view dreamwork as something sinful. They explore our rich heritage and the rightful legacy that each of us can enjoy without guilt. Fundamental Christians and those a little fearful of the process from a Judeo-Christian standpoint MUST read this book. The authors say, "Each night we let go, we die symbolically, not to nothingness, but to the rich and sometimes terrifying tapestry of the inner world. How can we adequately approach what we see there?" (p. 225) The book is the answer to that question with thirty-seven techniques for unraveling the mysteries. Since I don't consider dreams mysteries, the dreamwork portion of this book is for those who find my simple approach too modest for their tastes. If you want something to chew on intellectually, the techniques will intrigue you; and if you ever worried about the legitimacy of dreaming your way to God, this book will absolve you.

Search for God, A, Books I & II (Virginia Beach, Va.: A.R.E. Press, 1992)

A distillation of the wisdom contained in the Edgar Cayce readings concerning self-development. Covers such areas as meditation, cooperation, setting ideals, fellowship, patience, and love. Recommended for group use. This anniversary edition contains Books I and II (totalling twenty-four chapters).

Sechrist, Elsie. *Dreams: Your Magic Mirror* (New York: Warner Books, 1968)

Without a doubt, this is the best dream interpretation book ever written. Unfortunately it has gone out of print, but if enough people clamor for its re-issuance, we may convince the powers that be to put it into print again. Elsie has based her book on the Cayce readings, of which she was an ardent supporter. The book is a heartfelt, unpretentious presentation of every important aspect of dreaming, the process of interpretation, and the significance of application in daily living. She, like Cayce, emphasizes the spiritual content and the moral importance of each dream and each lessen therein. This book is a must for serious students of dreamwork and can be found in secondhand bookstores and by out-of-print book locators.

Twelve Steps and Twelve Traditions (New York: Alcoholics Anonymous World Services, Inc., 1952)

All 12 Steps and all traditions of the 12-Step programs are explored deeper than in the "Big Book." It is an excellent work on discussing principles and how to actually practice them in our lives. Although not a dream book, it certainly explains the process of living the lessons learned from dreamwork. I recommend it for anyone trying to apply spiritual lessons in everyday life.

Articles

Delaney, Gayle. "The Spiritual Dimension of Dreams." *Venture Inward* (January/February 1992), 37.

Huyghe, Patrick. "Dark Side of the Unknown." *Omni* (September 1993) 15:35-44, 81.

Pohle, Nancy. "Dream Insights: Waking Up to Who We Are." *Reflections* (October 1992), Vol. 1, No. 5: 1-4.

Remen, Rachael Naomi. "On Defining Spirit." *Noetic Sciences Review* (Fall 1993), 27:40.

Rosen, Daniel. "Interpret Your Life As a Dream." *Body Mind Spirit* (March/April 1994), 25, 67.

Sonera, Connie. "Dreams Work for Drug Addicts." *Venture Inward* (September/October 1990), 36-37.

Woodman, Marion. "Stepping over the Threshold." *Noetic Sciences Review* (Winter 1993), 10-15.

Workshop Material

The Course, Know Your Dreams and Know Yourself. Leader: Michael Karp, P. O. Box 1653, Big Bear Lake, CA 92315; (909) 866-7547.

Understanding Your Dreams. Leader: Ann Silverman, 7 Brill Crescent, Toronto, Ontario, Canada M2R 2X2; (416) 512-0725.

Interpret Life Events As a Dream. Leader: Robea, 292 Country Lane, Newport, WA 99156; (509) 327-6191.

Resource Directory

Adult Children of Alcoholics World Service Organization
P.O. Box 3216
Torrance, CA 90510
(310) 534-1815

Al-Anon Family Groups
P.O. Box 802, Midtown Station
New York, NY 10018
(800) 356-9996

Alcoholics Anonymous
Grand Central Station
P.O. Box 459
New York, NY 10163
(212) 870-3400

Co-Dependents Anonymous
P.O. Box 33577
Phoenix, AZ 80567-3577
(602) 277-7991

Narcotics Anonymous
P.O. Box 9999
Van Nuys, CA 91409-9999
(818) 780-3951

Women for Sobriety
P.O. Box 618
Quakertown, PA 18951-0618
(215) 536-8026

For help in finding or forming a mutual aid self-help group:

The Self-Help Sourcebook
Finding and Forming Mutual Aid Self-Help Groups
American Self-Help Clearinghouse
St. Clares Riverside Medical Center
Denville, NJ 07834
(201) 625-7101

Self-Help Canada
P.O. Box 64094
Ottawa, Ontario, Canada K1Y4V1
(613) 728-1865

Edgar Cayce Study Groups

A.R.E. Study Group Department
P.O. Box 595 (67th at Atlantic)
Virginia Beach, VA 23451-0595
(804) 428-3588

SYMBOLOGY INDEX
(For dreams only;
Standard Index follows)

Accessories, Glossary references and definitions of related words 104-106 (*see also* Appendix II)
Specific references in remaining text:
purse 139, 158, 159, 162
scarf 162
shoes 161
skate(s) 135

Air, Glossary references and definitions of related words 83 (*see also* Appendix II)
Specific references in remaining text:
air 133, 153
breathe 171
flying 19, 20, 151, 153, 175

Animals, Glossary references and definitions of many animals found in dreams 97-99 (*see also* Appendix II)
Specific references in remaining text:
animals (wild) 148, 170
cat 160
doe 22
dog(s) 30, 65
egg 173
lion 160
pet(s) 160
pig(s) 141
rabbit 152
reindeer 46
snake 68-69, 136, 138

Behavior (includes sex), Glossary references and definitions of activities 101-102 (*see also* Appendix II)
Specific references in remaining text:
accident 165
affair 28, 182
alone 143
argue, argument 141
breathe 133
chasing 66, 154, 155
clean(ing) 138-139, 155, 167

crash 136, 144, 145, 153
cut(ting) 134, 135
dance, dancing 138, 150
drinking 170
drive, driving 138, 144-145, 170
drown(ing) 149
drug abuse 21
eat(ing) 28, 29, 30, 71, 146, 151, 161
escap(ing) 68, 138
film 173
hug(ging) 173
kill(ing) 69, 157-158, 160, 163, 173 (*see also* "Death")
kiss(ing) 152
laugh(ing) 143-144, 176-178
love 72, 164, 166
peace 31
preparing food 28-30
sacrifice 151
sex(y) 32, 46, 70-71, 162, 168
shooting drugs 157-158, 166
skating 135
sleep(ing) 36
smiling 173
smoking 46, 133, 166
sob(bing) 152
sound 152
speeding 21, 23, 46
stealing 159
war 31
wash 156, 169
win 177

Birds, Glossary references and definitions of many birds found in dreams 97-98 (*see also* Appendix II)
Specific references in remaining text:
phoenix 85

Buildings, Glossary references and definitions of many buildings and related words found in dreams 121-123 (*see also* Appendix II)
Specific references in remaining

213

pot 136
rap song 25
rat poison 71-72
Saudi Arabia 175
South America 144, 180-181
Spanish 46
tickets 21, 23, 46
time warp 183
towel(s) 136-137
toy(s) 151, 162
TV 139, 158
urine 157
Uva Ursi tea 19
vabuti 48
vacation 171, 182
vodka 171

Plants, Glossary references and definition of plants (trees and foliage, can include plant food) 111-112 (*see also* Appendix II)
　Specific references in remaining text:
　banana 66-67
　cherries 66-67
　clover 151
　cranberries 19
　forest 148, 154
　tree(s) 134, 182, 183

Spiritual, Glossary references and definitions of spiritual and religious symbols found in dreams 119-120 (*see also* Appendix II)
　Specific references in remaining text:
　Angel of Darkness 150 (*see also* "Figures")
　birth 149
　Christ 28-30, 47, 77, 81, 145, 152, 162, 174, 182
　Christmas 46, 146
　cross 31, 131, 145, 153
　evil 33, 68, 136, 150
　heaven 31, 177
　hell 31
　Last Supper 151
　life 67
　Light 12
　Lucifer (*see also* "Figures")
　soul 179

temptation 68
Ying/Yang 147

Vehicles, Glossary references and definition of many vehicles 121-122 (*see also* Appendix II)
　Specific references in remaining text:
　bicycle 36
　BMW 136
　boat 143-144
　car 21, 32, 46, 138, 144, 183
　highway 134
　jeep 180
　motorcycle 134
　plane 19, 20, 175
　railroad tracks 170
　road 131, 134, 138
　roadblock 134
　roller coaster 148, 175
　spaceship(s) 133
　train(s) 148, 170

Water, Glossary reference and definition of related terms 81 (*see also* Appendix II)
　Specific references in remaining text:
　canal 143
　downpours 150
　hot tub 70
　hot water 70, 156
　lake 150
　ocean 138, 148
　puddle 156, 169
　river(s) 148
　snow 132, 150
　stream 138
　tempest(s) 148
　water 36, 71, 132, 138, 139, 156, 163
　wave(s) 149

STANDARD INDEX
(For dream symbols
see Symbology Index)

12 Steps: general 11-12; listed 44, 92-95, 199-200; objectives 45, 49-50, 66, 129

1st Step 137, 172-173

2nd Step 66, 138, 144, 145, 146, 147, 172-173

3rd Step 140, 147, 148, 149, 172-173

4th Step 47, 119, 138, 139, 140, 141, 144, 155, 165, 175

5th Step 15, 119, 139, 153, 154, 155, 165

6th Step 150, 151, 155, 165

7th Step 46, 153, 155, 156, 157, 158, 165

8th Step 67, 143, 155, 165

9th Step 67, 120, 153, 155, 158, 159, 160, 165

10th Step 139, 141, 152, 153, 155, 158, 160

11th Step 10, 47, 52, 152, 153

12th Step 160, 161, 162, 163, 164, 165

12-Step dreamwork group, benefits 55-56; guidelines 61, 63; purpose 72; traditions 58-59

12-Step dreamwork, appropriate for processing 49; definition of 14-15; purpose 41-42, 50, 72; setup 38, 49

12-Step programs 60; purpose 72; way of life 9-10

12-Step work, definition 14-15, 150, 155, 166

Adult Children of Alcoholics (ACOA), dreams from 141, 151, 152, 159, 164, 174, 175, 177, 181

Adult Children of Dysfunctional Families (ACDF), dreams from 149

akashic record 12, 24

Alanon 5, 60; dreams from 139, 144, 156

Alateen 159, 163, 183

Alcoholics Anonymous (AA), 9, 16, 19, 37, 55, 60, 70, 119, 162, 164, 167, 168, 172, 180; dreams from 131, 132, 133, 135, 137, 138, 140, 141, 143, 145, 146, 147, 150, 151, 152, 153, 154, 155, 159, 160, 161, 162, 164, 165, 167, 169, 170, 172, 174, 177, 180, 181; the book 9, 10, 11, 60 (*see also* "Big Book")

Allah 12, 13

angels 5, 9, 13 (*see also* "guardian angels"; "Figures" in Symbology Index)

A.R.E. study groups 55 (*see also* "Edgar Cayce study group")

Aristotelian 7

Aristotle 7, 8

astral travel 49, 83, 147, 153

astrology 91

atheist 131

Attention Deficit Disorder (ADD) 21, 184

auras 2

automatic writing 36

Bach, Richard 57

basic text 53, 119 (*see also* "Narcotics Anonymous")

Berne, Patricia H. 6

Bethards, Betty 10, 33, 34

Bible 5, 16, 53, 196

biblical characters: Boaz 6, Jesus the Christ 6, 12, 33, 59, 139, 145, 152, 153, 196 (*see also* "Spiritual" in Symbology Index), John the Baptist 9, Joseph 6, Mary 9, 139, 140, Moses 42, 85, Paul 6, 85, Pharoah 6, 8, Ruth 6, Zechariah 9

biblical reference(s) 51, by book: Acts 6, 16, Daniel 16, Deuteronomy 7, Ephesians 196, Genesis 6, 9, Leviticus 7, Luke 9, 33, Matthew 33, Numbers 16, Ruth 6

"Big Book" 9, 10, 39, 41, 50, 55, 119, 155, 180 (*see also* "Alcoholics Anonymous")

Book of Life 12

Bosnak, Robert 57

219

About the Author

Shelly Marshall is an intimate partner with overcoming adversity through spiritual growth. Her first great challenge in life was being reared in an alcoholic home, the second was her own addiction. In fact, the disease of addiction completely devastated her entire family and would have literally wiped them out if not for their mother's initial contact into recovery.

Ms. Marshall delved into dream interpretation, past lives, and other spiritual topics simultaneously with her 12-Step recovery. A spiritual experience led her to write her first book, *Day by Day,* which has since sold over two million copies. Subsequently Shelly has published five additional titles in both Russian and English—all devoted to spiritual growth. During recovery, Ms. Marshall earned a degree in human services, drug/alcohol and a degree in theology/counseling.

Today, this remarkable woman works around the world running addiction certification schools, conducting workshops, consulting for recovery treatment programs, and lecturing about spiritual growth through the 12-Step application.

What Is A.R.E.?

The Association for Research and Enlightenment, Inc. (A.R.E.®), is the international headquarters for the work of Edgar Cayce (1877-1945), who is considered the best-documented psychic of the twentieth century. Founded in 1931, the A.R.E. consists of a community of people from all walks of life and spiritual traditions, who have found meaningful and life-transformative insights from the readings of Edgar Cayce.

Although A.R.E. headquarters is located in Virginia Beach, Virginia— where visitors are always welcome—the A.R.E. community is a global network of individuals who offer conferences, educational activities, and fellowship around the world. People of every age are invited to partici- pate in programs that focus on such topics as holistic health, dreams, re- incarnation, ESP, the power of the mind, meditation, and personal spirituality.

In addition to study groups and various activities, the A.R.E. offers membership benefits and services, a bimonthly magazine, a newsletter, extracts from the Cayce readings, conferences, international tours, a mas- sage school curriculum, an impressive volunteer network, a retreat-type camp for children and adults, and A.R.E. contacts around the world. A.R.E. also maintains an affiliation with Atlantic University, which offers a master's degree program in Transpersonal Studies.

For additional information about A.R.E. activities hosted near you, please contact:

A.R.E.
67th St. and Atlantic Ave.
P.O. Box 595
Virginia Beach, VA 23451-0595
(804) 428-3588

A.R.E. Press

A.R.E. Press is a publisher and distributor of books, audiotapes, and videos that offer guidance for a more fulfilling life. Our products are based on, or are compatible with, the concepts in the psychic readings of Edgar Cayce.

We especially seek to create products which carry forward the inspira- tional story of individuals who have made practical application of the Cayce legacy.

For a free catalog, please write to A.R.E. Press at the address below or call toll free 1-800-723-1112. For any other information, please call 804- 428-3588.

A.R.E. Press
Sixty-Eighth & Atlantic Avenue
P.O. Box 656
Virginia Beach, VA 23451-0656

Discover for Yourself

the Wealth of Insights Contained in the Edgar Cayce Material...

Throughout his life, Edgar Cayce (1877-1945) was able to display powers of perception that extended beyond the five senses. He was guided by one solitary goal: to be helpful to people, and he used his talents of psychic perception to provide practical guidance for thousands of individuals.

The Edgar Cayce legacy contains information on more than 10,000 different subjects in the areas of healing, holistic health, spirituality, meditation, philosophy, reincarnation, dream interpretation, and prophecy. He has been called a philosopher, the most gifted psychic of all times, and the father of the holistic health movement. More than 300 books have been written about his work!

In 1931, Cayce founded the Association for Research and Enlightenment, Inc. (A.R.E.) to study and research this information. Today, the A.R.E. is an open-membership organization–made up of thousands of individuals around the world–that offers conferences, seminars, research projects, newsletters, and small group activities. For information, call 1-800-333-4499, or use the card below.

Enroll me as a member of A.R.E. (Edgar Cayce's Association for Research and Enlightenment, Inc.) I enclose $40.00 (Outside U.S.A. add $15.00 postage.)

VISA or Master Card CALL TOLL FREE
1-800-333-4499, 24 hours a day, 7 days a week

You may cancel at any time and receive a full refund on all unmailed benefits.

OR Make check or money order payable to A.R.E. (Non-U.S. residents must make payment in United States funds.)

❑ Check or Money Order   ❑ MasterCard   ❑ VISA

	Expiration Date		Charge Card Number

If payment is enclosed, please use envelope for your privacy.

Mo. | Yr.

1712

Signature_____
(Important! Sign here to use credit card.)

Name *(please print)* _____

Address _____

City_____ State _____ Zip _____

Phone (_____) _____

I can't join right now, but please send me additional information about A.R.E. activities, publications, and membership.

How Can I Participate in A.R.E.?

Although A.R.E. Headquarters is located in Virginia Beach, Virginia–where visitors are always welcome– the A.R.E. is a global network of individuals in more than seventy countries. The underlying principle of the Edgar Cayce readings is the oneness of all life, tolerance for all people, and a compassion and understanding for individuals of all faiths, races, and backgrounds.

In addition to Headquarters, hundreds of study groups and Edgar Cayce Centers exist world-wide. Regardless of your location, individuals are invited to participate in group activities, explore new publications, or simply enjoy membership benefits through the mail.

For additional information about the organization's activities and services, please use the card below or contact:

A.R.E., 67th Street & Atlantic Ave.
P.O. Box 595, Virginia Beach, VA 23451-0595

The Wealth of Insights Contained in the Edgar Cayce Material Includes:

Alternative Healing Principles	*Universal Laws*	*Global Community*
Dreams	*Attitudes & Emotions*	*ESP*
Spiritual Healing	*Mysticism*	*Self-Hypnosis*
Study Groups	*Karma & Grace*	*Death & Dying*
Earth Changes	*Meditation*	*Prophecy*
Psychic Development	*Spiritual Guidance*	*Astrology*
Atlantis & Ancient Civilizations	*Reincarnation*	*Akashic Records*
Discovering Your Soul's Purpose	*Angels*	*And Hundreds More. . .*

EDGAR CAYCE FOUNDATION and
A.R.E. LIBRARY/VISITORS CENTER
Virginia Beach, Virginia
Serving You Since 1931

NO POSTAGE
NECESSARY
IF MAILED
IN THE
UNITED STATES

BUSINESS REPLY MAIL
FIRST CLASS MAIL PERMIT NO. 2456, VIRGINIA

POSTAGE WILL BE PAID BY ADDRESSEE

A.R.E.®
P.O. Box 595
Virginia Beach, VA 23451-9989